logolounge 5

2,000 International Identities by Leading Designers

BEVERLY MASSACHUSETTS

ROCKPORT PUBLISHERS

Catharine Fishel and Bill Gardner

First published in the United States of America by
Rockport Publishers, a member of
Quayside Publishing Group
100 Cummings Center
Suite 406-L
Beverly, Massachusetts 01915-6101
Telephone: (978) 282-9590
Fax: (978) 283-2742
www.rockpub.com

Library of Congress Cataloging-in-Publication data
Fishel, Catharine M.

  LogoLounge 5 : 2,000 international identities by leading designers /
Catharine Fishel and Bill Gardner.

    p. cm.

  Includes index.

  ISBN-13: 978-1-59253-527-9

  ISBN-10: 1-59253-527-5

  1. Logos (Symbols) — Catalogs. 2. Corporate image — Catalogs. 3.
Designers — Directories. I. Gardner, Bill. II. Title. III. Title: Logo lounge five.

  NC1002.L63F57 2009

  741.6–dc22

                                                           2009001505

ISBN: 978-1-59253-735-8

10 9 8 7 6 5 4 3 2 1

Design: Gardner Design
Layout & Production: *tabula rasa* graphic design
Production Coordinator: Lauren Kaiser/Gardner Design
Cover Image: Gardner Design

Printed in Singapore

Thank you to all of the designers who for this and past books share so generously so that others can learn; to the Rockport team for its consistent support and structure; to Bill and the entire LogoLounge staff for their inspiration and guidance; to sons Alex, Andrew, and Sam for being my guiding lights and teachers; and to Denny, who makes every single day a pleasure and better than the one before.

—Catharine Fishel

To Brian, Cathy, Gail, and Troy, my LogoLounge cohorts and the brains of the brand.

To LogoLounge.com members worldwide for contributing over 100,000 logos to the site.

To Brian, Susan, Luke, Elisabeth, Ty, Jami, and Lauren for keeping Gardner Design ever genius.

To Andrea and Molly for making home a treat and retreat from designing and writing.

—Bill Gardner

contents

introduction

While at a recent conference in Moscow, I was drawn into a private conversation with an amazing brain trust of the world's top-tier brand strategists. It was a group dominated by planners and implementers, but shy on designers. With no clients within earshot, discussion centered on the inability of customers to maintain brand focus over the long term. Plans and strategies shift, brand managers move, ownership and products change—all make building consistency as easy as pushing a rope. "Where is the constant?" one professional asked.

Corporations go through the same changes that occur in countries around the world. Occasionally, there's a new leader with new policies, or political parties change, or new laws are created. But unless there's a full-scale revolution, the flag of the country pretty much stays the same. The constant is the logo.

Logo designers are the flag designers of the corporate world. When a brand stands ready to send a message to its public, you can be assured that it will be delivered with the corporate colors flying overhead.

Welcome to a book full of some pretty amazing flags. The designers who created the 2,000 logos in this book have a good grip on the process of boiling a concept down to its essence. They have created logos that brand loyalists and converts alike feel good about saluting. And as diverse as the content is, each mark speaks to its population because the designer is able to evoke an emotion or establish a mood without being overt or trite. The designer understands how to create an eloquent visual voice that is singular to the client.

Every branding or rebranding project has its own unique story that can only be comprehended by pulling back the sanitary public curtain and peering into the process. Journey here into the stories behind the story with case studies of the world's largest retailer, Walmart, or Australia's largest grocer, Woolworths. Explore development of the icon language for Apple's iPhone and the moving visual identity of telecommunication giant Swisscom. Read the story icons created for a Croatian Fairy Tale Festival, or flip forward to a new identity for the world's largest library, the Library of Congress.

Crossing broad cultures, the logos in this book were selected from more than 33,000 submissions from designers in over 100 countries around the world. An international panel of eight brand experts meticulously scrutinized and ranked these submissions to sift down to this amazing collection. Each winning logo was categorized in this book to create a logical and seamless resource.

Your ability to efficiently sort through thousands of logos is a hallmark of www.LogoLounge.com. The site contains more than 100,000 logos to date, contributed by thousands of international members. These members represent the brightest designers from the largest of top-tier firms to the smallest shops in nearly every country on Earth.

It's never been easier for clients and designers to make connections than through this book or through LogoLounge.com. The site allows any member to quickly search an immense database for reference, inspiration, or contacts. Finding relevant content is as easy as entering a simple keyword, industry, style, client, designer, design firm, date range, or other term.

New features make visual searching even quicker and more intuitive, and lightboxes allow the user to easily sort and organize content for convenient access. Every membership also allows the user to upload his or her own work to be considered for inclusion in the next volume of the LogoLounge book series.

Sample a bit of the site for free by logging into www.logolounge. com/book5, where you can search through the logos from this book using the same tools our full members use to peruse the world's largest searchable collection of logos. Learn more about the 2,000 flags that are flying higher than any other today.

—Bill Gardner

jurors

Alex de Jánosi
Lippincott, New York, New York

Gartenwelt Manz, by Kommunication & Design
"This is not an easy task to review [all of the LogoLounge submissions]: After all, there are only so many Michael Schwab rip-offs one can handle! I much admire the symbol for the nursery Gartenwelt Manz. Even though we can find similar mosaics in modern art and, of course, the Altria logo is akin, this mark is quite appropriate, unique, and memorable for a garden nursery. I like it for a number of reasons:

• *It does not rely on the overused leaf, vine, or tree symbol found in 99.9 percent of other nursery logos.*
• *The color palette used in the symbol is beautiful.*
• *The visual system extension or graphic language you can extract from the symbol for boxes, pots, planters, and advertisements would be wonderful.*

A successful garden conveys a rich variety and hierarchy of colors and shades, patterns, and textures. This logo represents just that in a thoughtful, elegant, and unique way."

Alex de Jánosi is a design partner with more than 15 years' experience developing major corporate identity

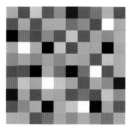

GARTENWELT
ΜΑΝΖ

programs for U.S. and international organizations, from Rio to Riyadh, and places in between.

De Jánosi has been responsible for designing logos and overseeing print, Web, and environmental design development and management for a wide range of clients.

His work has been featured in leading design publications and books on corporate identity. De Jánosi holds a B.F.A. in graphic design from the Philadelphia College of Art (University of the Arts).

Vince Frost
Frost Design, Sydney, Australia

San Antonio Zoo, by Bradford Lawton Design Group
"My selection really doesn't need an explanation as it's an effortless typographic illustration that makes you smile. It's a clever observation which turns two simple numbers and two basic colors into a distant relative."

Vince Frost is principal and creative director of Frost Design, a 30-person studio based in Sydney, Australia, offering a diverse mix of talents—from graphic and multimedia designers to architects, interior designers, and brand strategists who work on a wide range of projects, including magazine and book design to corporate identity, environmental graphics, and interactive design, Frost's approach is all about coming up with exceptional ideas, based on listening carefully to the needs of each client and then coming up with a bespoke solution-making each project the very best it can be.

Frost has led the rebranding of the Sydney Opera House; broadcast and identity design for Channel [V]; the new logo for Mushroom Records; a new identity and campaigns for Sydney Dance Company; the advertising campaign for Australia's Northern Territory; the redesign of *Australian Creative* magazine; the design of *French* cookbook for Penguin; and environmental graphics and identities for Manta and Coast restaurants. He is a member of CSD, D&AD, ISTD, AGDA, and AGI. Frost plays an active role in the world design community, lecturing at colleges and conferences.

Andreas Karl
Karl Design-Marken für Morgen,
Vienna, Austria

Yellowstone Holiday, by Scott Sorenson of Axiom Collaborative

"After viewing more than 6,000 logo designs, I finally ended up with 250 very good ones. And this logo is the favorite of my favorites. At the first glimpse you might say: 'Okay . . . a moose.' But look longer! A little bit closer! Now you see it too. Why have I chosen it for my judge's choice? I generally like clever logos with animals, but this wasn't the point here. This design is a good example of a piece of work you cannot generate on a computer in a few minutes. You have to concentrate on every single detail. Each component must be adjusted by hand and compared in size and position until the result has the right proportions to form the horns of a moose. I would be proud if I had created this moose myself. A brilliant idea and a perfect illustration: You must not change a single line. This logo was done by an artist who sees nature in a different way. The quality of this mark is its hidden mystery, the things you don't see. For us viewers it is like falling in love at the second sight. But once we have discovered the two other animals in this logo, the picture sticks in our memory forever.

Andreas Karl has studied visual communication and arts in Wuerzburg, Germany. A freelance illustrator for publishers and children's books in his first working years, Karl became more and more focused on logo design. From 1991, he worked as an art director and later creative director doing branding, packaging, and corporate design for many angencies, and in 2001, he founded his own studio in Frankfurt named Karl Design—Marken Für Morgen (now of Austria).

Jamie Koval
VSA Partners, Chicago, Illinois

Sink, by Zoe Design Associates

"When evaluating an identity, I try to look at it purely from a conceptual and visual perspective. That said, it is often difficult to avoid imagining what the personality of the company is, how the identity looks in application, or how their products are designed, and what messaging runs parallel with this symbol. All that aside, Sink is my choice. It was a solution that had a well-executed idea. I appreciate the simplicity and boldness. I like the modern/retro, industrial/playful quality of this identity."

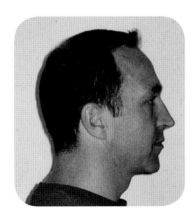

Jamie Koval joined VSA Partners as a creative director and partner in 1990. In 2002, he was named president of the firm and helped redefine the firm's integrated approach to communication. Koval's success is marked by his ability to combine creative and strategic thinking as well as bring clarity to multifaceted programs that include corporate communications, brand identity, advertising, marketing communications, and interactive.

Koval has worked on projects for Adidas, BP, Cingular, The Coca-Cola Company, and Gap, to name a few. He has contributed and led creative workshops for brands such as Starbucks and Leo Burnett and has designed a stamp for the U.S. Postal Service.

His talent for design has been recognized nationally and internationally, and his work is part of the permanent collection in the Library of Congress in Washington, D.C.

Sarah Moffat
Turner Duckworth, San Francisco, California

Minus Mineral Water, by Scott Stemke of La Visual
"Many of the entries seemed over-complicated and over-embellished, but Minus keeps things simple. This logo rose to the top demonstrating the adage that less is indeed more."

Sarah Moffat was raised and educated in England and graduated from Kingston University with a design honors degree in 1998. Moffat's creative talent has been acknowledged by multiple industry and peer awards for client projects such as Waitrose, Superdrug, Cadbury Schweppes, Homebase, Virgin Atlantic, Coca-Cola, and The Royal Mail. After working for eight years in Turner Duckworth's London studio, she moved across the Atlantic to become the San Francisco studio's design director. She is responsible for creative direction, and all strategic and design output from the San Francisco studio, from award-winning work for entrepreneurial clients such as Click Wine Group (Root:1, Bootleg, and Fat bastard) to cultural influencer brands such as Coca-Cola (Coke Zero, Coca-Cola, and Diet Coke visual identity systems).

Bronwen Rautenbach
The Brand Union, Johannesburg,
South Africa

Gift of Love, by Pictogram Studio
"This piece of work, done for a gift shop, has an honesty and immediacy that I found refreshing. It explains the act of giving so well. The crafting and characterization has a rawness to it which contributes to its power. I believe a good logo captures the spirit of a brand. This is not just a gift shop: It is a place that has insight into our human condition. I guess at the end of it, after all the thousands of logos I looked at, this is the one that moved me most and for that reason it gets my vote."

Bronwen Rautenbach is an identity, visual language, and art direction specialist, with a love for design in the broadest sense of the word. She has a particular obsession with logos.

Rautenbach began her career in 2000 with a brief flirtation in corporate design at Graphicor, a company specializing in annual reports and editorial. She then joined the Switch group in 2001, where she spent three years. She joined the Brand Union in 2004 as a senior designer, was promoted to design director in 2006, and to creative director in 2007.

Michelle Sonderegger
Design Ranch, Kansas City, Missouri

Water Wise, by Chad Worth

"This logo is a unique play on form and typography. Mirroring the water droplet is reflective of a lightbulb, which says 'think.' It visually reinforces the concept of water conservation. The typography used to create the face is lighthearted and brings a human element to the design, which is also important to the concept. The use of lowercase typography and soft edges is friendly and approachable. The simplicity of the mark works

well because it clearly communicates the message of the company."

Michelle Sonderegger is a founding partner of Design Ranch, one of the top graphic design firms in the Midwest. Her work specializes in innovative, strategic, and visual communication solutions for clients ranging from start-ups to Fortune 500 corporations such as Buckle, Dell, H&R Block, Hallmark, Payless ShoeSource, Lee Jeans, and Target.

Design Ranch has been featured in several national and international publications such as *Novum, Communication Arts, Graphis,* and *Print.* The firm has received awards from respected institutions such as the American Advertising Federation, American Institute of Graphic Arts, and Type Directors Club.

In 2005, Design Ranch launched a product line featuring three exclusive brands: Design Ranchables, Meangirl, and Pantease. The products include T-shirts, underwear, notecards, and giftables. Characterized by visual impact and humor, the products have been featured on Target's Red Hot Shop and highlighted in *Teen Vogue.*

Von Glitschka
Glitschka Studios, Portland, Oregon

Human rights protest, by Andreas Karl

"Normally, politically motivated design doesn't do much for me. But when I saw this mark in response to the 2008 Olympics, I thought it was high-concept brilliance. Profoundly simple in its execution, but simply profound in its message. Not an easy thing to do."

Von Glitschka has worked in the communication arts industry for more than 20 years. He now refers to himself as an illustrative designer. In 2002, he started Glitschka Studios, a multidisciplinary creative firm.

His work reflects the symbiotic relationship between design and illustration, thus his modus operandi is that of a hired gun for both in-house art departments and medium to large creative agencies working on projects for such clients as Microsoft, Adobe, Pepsi, Rock and Roll Hall of Fame, Major League Baseball, Hasbro, Bandai Toys, John Wayne Foundation, Merck, Allstate Insurance, Disney, Lifetime Television and HGTV.

He also teaches advanced digital illustration at Chemeketa Community College and operates the website IllustrationClass.com where visitors can download tutorials documenting his illustrative design process on a variety of diverse project types.

portraits

Design Firm	Lippincott
Client	Walmart
Project	Corporate Identity Redesign

When most large companies get a new logo or rebrand, it's primarily a matter of interest for their own staff, and secondarily, for their customers. On the third tier, perhaps, is the design press and the design community. But usually, it isn't national or international news.

Word of Walmart's rebranding sparked an entirely different reaction. Its new logo—called the "spark"—was an overnight sensation. The Internet, national news services, newspapers, and magazines covered the new mark. Everyone, it seemed, was wondering: Where would Wal-Mart—now Walmart—go next?

> Now the company wanted to move more toward the benefit it gave customers—the emotional benefit

As the leading retail chain in the United States, Walmart is bound to make waves when it makes such a major decision. But the exceptional public and press reaction had less to do with the news of the redesign than it did with how it affected people personally. Some were unsure; others were intrigued. And that's exactly the connection Walmart hoped to convey through the new identity: Affect people in a personal, one-on-one way. As its new motto proclaims, "Saving people money so they can live better."

"The key aspect of Walmart was stated in its previous motto: 'Always low prices. Always.' Their purpose has always been to save people money. But now the company wanted to move more toward the benefit it gave customers—the emotional benefit," says Su Mathews, senior partner with Lippincott, the design office who worked with Walmart for nearly two years to develop the new identity, brand positioning, and the store environment that supports both.

When the chain was founded in 1962, Walmart was a five-and-dime store serving rural areas. It offered the least expensive goods. Today, with almost 7,400 stores in the United States and abroad, it has enormous buying clout and a solid understanding of its current and soon-to-be customers. It offers everything from car repair, jewelry, and groceries to gasoline, goldfish, and electronics. A customer can run in for a pack of gum or an enormous flat-screen TV and be relatively certain that the price will be the best around. If customers save money, and their shopping experience is clean, simple, and quick, the company reasons, their lives will be made easier. Saving

Top: Walmart's new identity contains a new word mark—minus the hyphen—and a new logo, called "the spark." Lippincott was the design office that worked with Walmart for nearly two years to develop the new identity, brand positioning, and the store environment that supports both.

Above: Walmart's old logo was familiar to shoppers, but it did not have the friendly, customer-service-centered feel that its management wanted to communicate. The old star symbol also was not particularly ownable. In fact, many other retail stores use stars in their identities.

A limited edition, hardcover brand book explains the history and evolution of the company, again using the new identity in its design.

money at Walmart allows people to afford more and spend elsewhere in their lives.

Today, Walmart continues to look for ways to offer customers a more complete shopping experience. One example is its expansion into financial services, by providing money centers for customers to perform transactions such as check cashing. Another area is pharmacy, which offers the best prices and saves shoppers a trip to the drugstore. Walmart also offers a "site-to-store" program to enable customers to shop online for a broad assortment of items and have these shipped directly to their local store for pick-up-free of shipping charges.

All of this growth had moved Walmart past its previous hyphenated, low-emotion identity with embedded star, which had been developed in 1992. The company needed a more proprietary, less U.S.-centric mark that spoke more about the innovation and greater benefit it was now able to offer not just to customers, but also to its employees and the communities it served at home and abroad.

"The star in the old logo is a very generic symbol," explains Mathews. "It does have a sense of patriotism, but it's not really ownable. Other stores use a star in their identities, so it just wasn't that unique. It also wasn't a symbol that could be used separately, away from the word mark, and still be recognizable as Walmart."

Initially, Walmart looked to Lippincott for help in assessing the goals of the brand to determine if a logo update might better support its objectives. But as the client and design team continued to work together, it became clear that the emotional quotient could be significantly improved with a clean break to something new.

The team determined that Walmart's core personality traits were caring, real, innovative, and straightforward. This pointed toward a new identity that was more human and warm, one that showed how everyone who worked and shopped at the store was treated with respect. The new identity needed to convey service through the provision of quality products in a clean, simple manner.

The Lippincott team considered a wide range of ideas. Some were outside of the client's initial comfort range, while others were very close to the 1992 mark. In developing the design, the team reviewed a wide range of concepts. As Walmart competes with a broad set of retailers, the designers needed to consider word mark options used classically in home and apparel, and iconic symbols used more commonly by supermarkets, for example. Some exploratory directions emphasized a sense of community, to reflect that Walmart is a place where people come together for a variety of needs. Other exploratory directions more heavily spoke to Walmart's sustainability efforts. Some playful and fun design directions

It became clear that the emotional quotient could be significantly improved with a clean break to something new.

communicated the "low cost" message in a more lighthearted way, with imagery inspired by price tags.

In the end, the team rejected several directions as being too literal or singularly focused. As the retailer continues to evolve, it needs an identity that can similarly "stretch." It would have mass appeal, but not fade quickly or become commonplace. In its simplicity, it would communicate in a straightforward and direct manner-almost as a pictogram does. They decided on the spark.

The spark concept at first was a bit more challenging for the client, but one that had an aspirational quality that everyone liked. Different shapes and designs for the spark were considered—using different numbers of spokes and various colors, for instance—but the very simple design that was eventually chosen felt human, warm, and very to-the-point. It speaks of inspiration and of good ideas.

"The spark is really about the idea of being smart. There is a great emotional benefit for people when they feel smart about what they buy. The spark is like the lightbulb going off over your head. It's like a spark of empowerment and of living better," Mathews says. "It is visualizing the thought that 'I would be crazy to go somewhere else and spend more.'"

The new symbol has also turned out to mean different things to different people. Some see it as a burst of energy, or as a sun, flower, or firework. Others see it as a *W* over an *M*. It might also be seen as the spark of inspiration customers feel when they leave the store, or the spark of inspiration and innovation that helps the company and employees find new ways to save people money, or even the spark of inspiration that moved founder Sam Walton to open his first store.

"Different people see different things in the symbol, and this enables the spark to communicate across a wide spectrum of categories, from tires to apparel, and from home goods to fresh food," she adds.

The new logo is more flexible than the old star. For instance, it can be used as a half-spark above a person's head in a photo or above a product in an ad to signal a good idea. If placed before a word or phrase, it introduces a smart concept. Placed after, it is a sort of punctuation that lends emphasis. In animation, it can burst out, like a good idea.

"The animation did need to support the idea that it was a spark and not a flower or something else," Mathews says.

The other components of the identity system support the spark and the client's messaging. In addition to the half-spark, "talk boxes" (which are like word bubbles, but square) are used to call out smart messages or display quotes.

Walmart's new photography scheme is very warm and human. The brand guidelines say the photography must support the key messages; be of high quality; reflect a positive emotional benefit; and support the key personality traits of the Walmart brand.

Matthew Larsen
**Sr. Manager,
Advertising & Brand Strategy**

702 Southwest 8th St.
Bentonville, AR 72716-0310
T 479.204.6864   M 479.366.6404
T 479.204.1234   M 479.366.5678
matt.larsen@wal-mart.com

Other pieces in the new
Walmart identity system.

The company's new color
scheme is built around three
blues: The medium and light
blue are brighter and friendlier
than those used in the previous identity. The deepest blue
is a clear, strong tone. The
system also includes a bright
orange-red, a grass green, and
a darker green.

The system's logotype and other copy is set in Myriad Pro. It, too, feels warm and humanistic, with friendly curves in its letterforms. It also has a modern sensibility. Because of its simple nature, it suggests easy shopping and low price.

"We use a bold, a light, and a book," Mathews explains. "The light is used for apparel or items for the home, more fashion-forward products. Book and bold are used for the basics. The cut of the book and bold weights work well for body copy and signage or store navigation."

Finally, the new Walmart identity system is built around three blues: The medium and light blue are brighter and friendlier than those used in the previous identity. The deepest blue is a clear, strong tone. In addition to being the mainstay color of the old identity, blue is most people's favorite color, says Mathews. It is also perceived as familiar, loyal, and trustworthy.

The system also includes a bright orange-red, a grass green, and a darker green. Yellow in retail use is emblematic of low cost, so the Lippincott designers selected a richer yellow to balance the ideas of low cost and quality. All of these colors work well in the food, grocery, meat, and bakery areas. It is a fresh palette, with plenty of vibrancy. The overall effect, especially inside the stores, is much warmer than the old blue-on-blue, under-fluorescent-lights system.

The old word mark, previously set in all caps, was strident and heavy. To produce a more welcoming look, the client's name is now set in caps and lowercase. Changing the name to one word was a simple way to make the name more a crest of quality, not a contrived word. It also helps aid perception: It is easier and quicker to read as one word.

One curious aspect to the final design of the logo and word mark together is that it is actually being used in smaller sizes on signage than the old combo. With the new spark, signage just does not need to be as large.

"They don't have to scream with the logo anymore, because now they have the symbol. People now can read the identity by its unique shape, which includes the spark. It is a new way of looking at Walmart," Mathews says.

United Motor Works

Identity Design, Lippincott, Hong Kong, China

What began as an auto repair shop in Singapore in 1917 has today grown into UMW, a RM8.4 billion (almost $2.5 billion U.S.) conglomerate engaged in four core businesses: automotive; heavy, industrial, and materials-handling equipment, and stand-alone engines for power generation; manufacturing and engineering; and oil and gas. The UMW (United Motor Works) is a strong brand name in Malaysia, but its management wanted customers everywhere to understand that the company was much more than the automotive division, which many people knew through UMW's long-term relationship with Toyota.

In fact, the company's move into oil and gas was its most significant recent expansion. To help signal the group's growth and to provide a catalyst with which to reinvigorate the company's internal structure, a new identity would be necessary.

The original UMW logo was a graphical representation of the Chinese characters *hé* and *shün,* meaning "united" and "collaboration," respectively. Both were words that UMW wanted to reinforce. One of the characters in particular also inspired the designer.

"The idea of smooth flow in one direction, contained in the character *shün* gave me inspiration for the initial sketches, around a dynamic letter *U* made up of multiple parts moving in sync," explains Vincenzo Perri, partner and creative director for Asia for Lippincott, from his office in Hong Kong. Lippincott was the agency of record for the project.

New logo design

Old logo design

Although other directions were explored, the *U* shape was soon recognized as the concept with the most possibilities. The letter represented the word *united,* of course, but the word and letter also stated exactly what management wanted: for the company to become a strong and harmonious group, to become united.

Perri played with a variety of kinetic shapes, combining many small pieces and uniting them in the U shape. "The shapes clearly express the change and transformation taking place at UMW and captured the idea of dynamic enterprise. Multiple shapes coming together also reflected the diverse lines of business working together toward a common goal," Perri says.

Vibrant color was part of all of the team's explorations. The color is very active and seems to produce a sense of motion. It also expresses the rich colors of Asia, Perri adds, as well as the varied cultural and ethnic mix inside the group.

The final logo contains at its center what some people see as a droplet. While Perri sees this as a positive association to the company's growth in oil, it is not an aspect that they give much emphasis.

"The shape came about as we were refining the logo because we had to avoid using sharp corners and shapes which carry negative connotations in feng shui," he says. "As the stems of the *U* expand upward, they close the negative space. Closed shapes are perceived as having better feng shui, which is an important consideration in Asia."

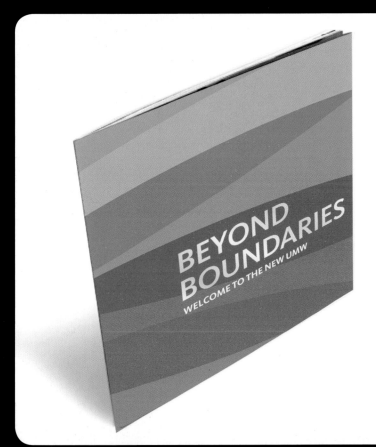

The word mark portion of the logo is made of custom-drawn letters with proportions that are relative to the typeface Kievit, which was selected as the corporate font for the entire identity program. The designers adjusted the weight of the letters to provide a good base for the symbol and changed the *M* to be more visually differentiated from the *W*. This improved legibility created a more unified appearance in the brand name.

Design Firm	Felix Sockwell
Client	New York Times
Project	Identity icons for iPhone users

For all its bells and whistles and oohs and aahs, the iPhone has the same screen as most other phones—smallish, with limited resolution—only 163 ppi. With that in mind, it's easy to understand the challenge a designer would face in designing a set of 30 icons that would somehow communicate the contents of the *New York Times* to iPhone users through the tiny screen.

Such GUI projects are more and more common these days: Each presents special challenges. Designer Felix Sockwell is a master of the reduction necessary to cull art to its most basic form while blessing it with the personality of the project and client at hand. His collection of thirty, 29 x 29-pixel icons deliver just the facts, yet behave in the elegant yet lively manner of the "Old Gray Lady," the *Times*.

It was an interesting project, said Sockwell. Working with the *Times'* Web wizard Khoi Vinh and design director Caryn Tutine, he produced many trials

> I had to think about each icon for a long time trying to find the most obvious solution.

for each section, trying to make each communication as simple and direct as possible. It was very unlike a traditional logo project where a design is usually replete with meaning and/or symbolism.

"I had to think about each icon for a long time," he says, "trying to find the most obvious solution. It's hard to pick just one object to represent something like sports, so some designs took a while. Also, keeping the language consistent was a challenge. In the end, some are 2-D and some are 3-D."

Each icon is a curious puzzle for a designer: The finished drawing must be readable in a fraction of a second, but not be a cliché. It must convey information forcefully, but not be so strong (in humor, style, history, or whatever) that it becomes a distraction. And, of course, what might seem like the perfect icon in the designer's mind may not hold as much resonance for the client: Like all design, judgment is subjective. So back-and-forthing can be a bit more likely.

Designs for GUI projects have some similarities. A finished set must have a familial feel—that is, simply look like they go together. That means that as the entire group is developed, certain designs—previously okay—will have to be reworked or even discarded to maintain the aesthetic.

The NYT's icon set lives well in the existing iPhone environment.

Another similarity is that any object considered for an icon must be very simple in form. For example, Sockwell notes that a water bottle would likely not be a good icon: Its form is too complicated, and the bottle shape isn't instantly ownable by the water market. A bottle could represent almost any drink.

Sockwell begins each icon by carefully considering the category it should represent, then selecting a few images that might be representative—a shoe for fashion, for instance. Then he heads online and pulls up plenty of images of fashionable shoes. He creates outlines from these and studies them to see which are working best. From there, it's an exercise in reduction—but not too much.

"I was very happy with the economy of these icons," Sockwell says. "But there are details in there that could be one single pixel that makes the drawing better. Ninety percent of people would not want to think of or notice the details. If as a designer you aren't into details, this will be a rough process for you."

It's the details that rescue the icons from bland. Still, the goal of the GUI icon is the same as a road sign: to get people where they want to go.

"The goal is to stay out of the way and let the icon just communicate," the designer says.

Sockwell has provided explorations for a number of the icons he created for the iPhone project to illustrate his process. The red circles indicate the chosen solutions; notes were added by Sockwell.

Art and Business Sockwell began the project with the art, business, latest news, and dining icons (latter two not shown here). The contrast between the art and business designs shows how some ideas come easily, whereas others are more difficult. The artist's palette is a clear and recognizable symbol: It was simply a matter of selecting the right amount of detail for the final art. The business concept, on the other hand, was more elusive: What said "business"? Sockwell feels that the final solution is one of the most successful in the group.

"The squareness of the business icon has a bit more weight on the page. It also reads on two levels: First, you see a square or circle shape, then you see there is something inside of it. You can read that very quickly. Compare that to the black-and-white hands: It just takes longer to read that icon and understand what it is," he explains.

Real Estate and Automobiles The real estate and automobile icons show how one icon can influence another. Both designs had myriad possibilities, as Sockwell's trials show. In some trials for real estate, the designer tried to communicate different sorts of housing/buildings, and in others, he wanted to suggest "home" through the addition of a tree. In the end, the client wanted to be iconic. The designer kept the design interesting, though, by adding a suggestion of a roofline and opening door.

That decision influenced the automobile design, which also had plenty of possibilities. It also ended up being more flat, with just a touch of detail.

Politics The designer says that the client was very interested in the elephant/donkey design, but eventually decided it had perhaps a bit too much humor. "Using the capitol dome is undeniably Washington, and therefore, politics," he says.

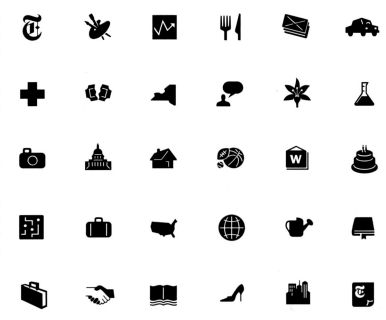

Felix Sockwell worked with *New York Times'* Web wizard Khoi Vinh and design director Caryn Tutine to create a *Times* GUI for the iPhone. The simplicity of the icons belies the complicated nature of the project.

for Arts

for Business

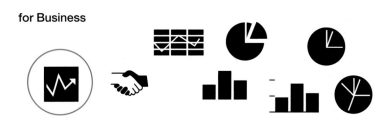

for Opinion

Sports Because there are so many sports, this icon proved tough: What one symbol could say it all? Sockwell felt that the whistle was a good, nondenominational symbol. But even though the three balls that were eventually selected clearly do not represent all sport, in the public mind, they do identify the category easily.

Health Initially, the design team felt that the caduceus would be an ideal symbol to represent health. In terms of its information value, it was excellent. But in its graphical form, it proved to be a bit too complicated. The universal first aid symbol would be better for the GUI.

Opinion Sockwell preferred the solutions that showed two contrasting opinions through two talk bubbles. He felt that the chosen solution creeps very slightly into the area of chat. But the client felt that this solution felt solid and more like the rest of the family.

U.S. The symbol for the U.S. reveals how attention to minute detail is crucial in icon design. "These are png [portable network graphics] files. You have to draw them really big and zoom up and down on them to figure out the details," Sockwell says.

Home and Garden Sometimes a category that seems simple turns out to be broader than expected. For the home and garden icon, Sockwell imagined using a watering can. But when he researched the topic, he found a very wide range of styles. He decided that an older model was more iconic.

Jobs The jobs icon proved to be one of the toughest challenges. Showing classified ads in such a tiny format didn't work, and ideas like the writing hand or megaphone didn't really communicate the category. Eventually, the briefcase won out, although the designer did not feel that it represented "jobs" well. "Most people don't carry briefcases anymore, and not all jobs are white collar," he points out.

City The city icon presents a good lesson in designer economics. Because there are many icons in each system he works on, Sockwell must be conservative with the time he spends on each. The city icon trials contain plenty of detail, and therefore, presented plenty of opportunity for reworking. In order to make money, doodling must be limited.

Obituaries The process toward a solution for the obituaries icon was perhaps the most contentious. Sockwell felt strongly that the gravestone said it all; a coffin might also do the trick. But the client found those solutions too morbid. So the designer experimented with placing a flower in front of the stone. Still, no go. A lily was the final solution. "I think it's ludicrous," the designer says, "but it is up to the client. You can only show what you think is right and try to sell it."

for Automobiles

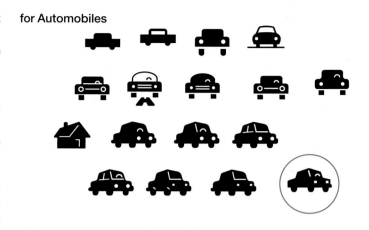

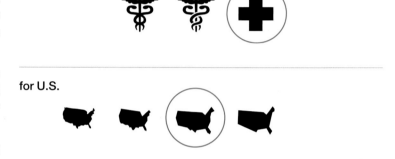

for Health

for U.S.

for Real Estate

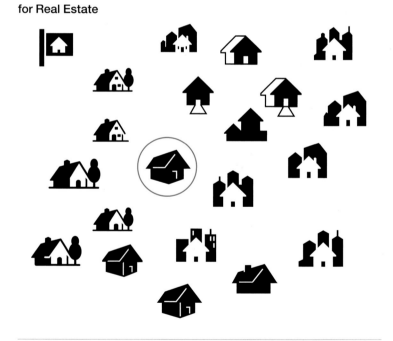

for Home + Garden

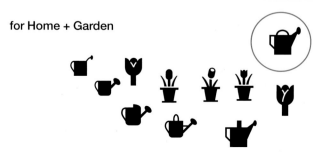

for Politics

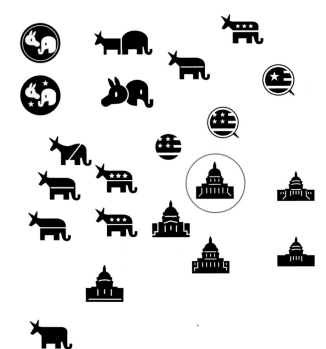

for City

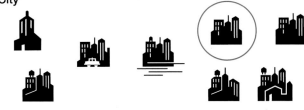

for Fashion + Style

for Most E-Mailed

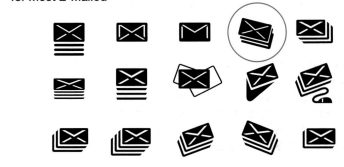

for Sports

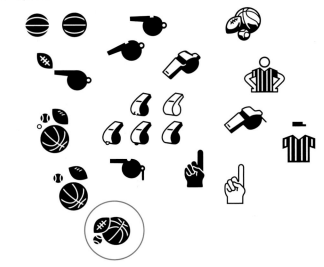

for Travel

for Jobs

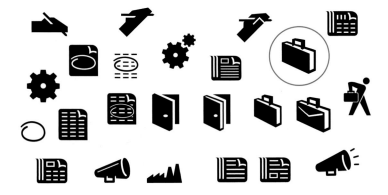

for Obituaries

United States Holocaust Memorial Museum
Identity Design

Felix Sockwell, Maplewood, New Jersey

A client whose work is as charged with emotion as the United States Holocaust Memorial Museum needs an identity that speaks plainly of its charge but which does not attempt to add fuel to anyone's fire. The identity must itself be emotionless, but through its design, inform, educate, and empathize.

Felix Sockwell (Maplewood, N.J.) was one of about ten designers/design firms invited to pitch the identity for the organization. The invitation was a rigorous one: Each invitee had to share three past jobs for which they had been paid more than $50,000 and provide all of the museum contact information fee structuring on those jobs. "Given the strict guidelines, I knew I didn't stand a chance," says Sockwell.

Regardless, he pulled together what he could, teaming with Stefan Sagmeister to build the proposal. Sockwell was certain he would not get the job but was still intrigued with the project, as was Sagmeister. After sending in the paperwork and portfolios, Felix and pal Thomas Fuchs met at a local bar and sketched over conversation.

"We were just in awe of the challenge of the whole thing," Sockwell recalls. "What could you actually do? It's such a huge challenge. We stopped talking and began thinking on the back of a big envelope."

Although the USHMM does represent survivors through exhibits and education, a new focus has been to witness and prevent genocide today. It represents all victims. One of the museum's main goals was to attract younger patrons. It also wanted to make all possible visitors and patrons more aware that the museum was not simply a repository for history, but that it was strenuously advocating for the future.

The day after sketching with Fuchs, Sockwell pulled out the sketches and began reworking them, a process that would continue over several weeks.

"It was a subject that had to be treated respectfully. A new design would have to be evocative, emotive, and dynamic so that younger people would feel expression in it," he explains.

One concept that Sockwell liked was a candle flame that sat upon a candle shape formed by the words in the name of the client. In its simplest iteration, this design used an actual flame.

"I liked the idea that the words made the candle. One of the things they do every year at the museum is light a holocaust candle. This is a nice way to think about it and be reminded—better to light a candle than to curse the darkness," he says.

It was a potent emotional device, one that also could be played out in marketing. The museum could sell candles in honor or memory of specific people or events, and the monies could be used to support the museum.

Growing from this basic idea, another concept superimposed the simple shape of an eye across a line drawing of a flame. Inside of the eye and flame was the image of a dove. The designer also played with a design that settled a dove at the base of a flame. These were sturdy statements, he believed, but perhaps too charged.

The Star of David design that eventually became the submission he sent to the USHMM committee combined symbols of oppressive power (upside-down triangle), and literal translations of land, water, flame, hand, and a dove. He began the design with the upside-down triangle on the right, a powerful symbol that, in this context, speaks of the tenuous balance of peace. He proceeded around the star clockwise, continuing to alter and transform each triangle in subtle, meaningful ways.

"I like this mark because it lacks emotion. It's all science. Facts. Yet its contents are really bold. There is no whimsy in it. It was trimmed back quite a bit after about 40 or 50 versions. I couldn't stop working on it. It was insane. I had to figure this thing out before my head exploded. It became personal," Sockwell says.

Although he eventually lost the assignment to Pentagram's Paula Scher, Sockwell had no regrets about the project. In fact, he says, it was invigorating. "It was nice to lose to Paula. I have a lot of respect for who she is and what she does."

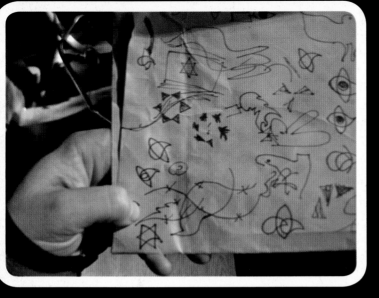

Sketches that Felix Sockwell, Thomas Fuchs, and Stefan Sagmeister created in their explorations of the museum logo.

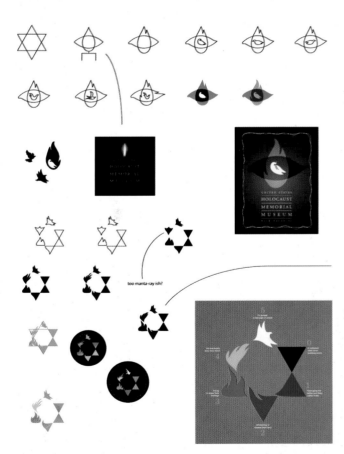

too manta-ray ish?

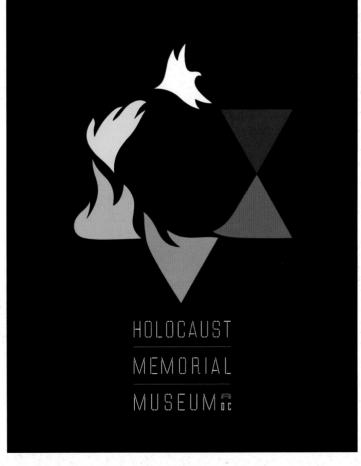

HOLOCAUST
MEMORIAL
MUSEUM DC

The final proposal (at right), with other explorations.

Design Firm	Fragile
Client	Alias
Project	Identity Redesign

A fashion-forward client needs an identity with long legs, as well as an eternally youthful body that can be dressed and redressed, season after season, and always be in style.

Such was the case for Alias, an Italian firm famous for its innovative approach to furniture design. Every year, the company produces an entirely new line of furniture that must have an entirely new identity in order to be marketed properly. But the company's own core identity needs to remain intact—recognizable and solid—all of the time.

"Changes occur rapidly for our client, according to fashion, production, new stores, or the partner's ideas. They need a common frame for the company identity, but a very elastic, prompt response to outside influences," says Mario Trimarchi, principal of Fragile, the Milan-based design

> The water bottle is a commodity, but it is also an archetype: It has proven to be long-lasting in our lives.

firm that has worked with Alias since 1999 to keep its identity fresh and relevant. "Every season we change something in the communication for that year's design."

Alias' products are highly designed, down to the smallest details: Unconventional use of commonplace material, such as polyester mesh and extruded aluminum, has been carefully considered and crafted. Invention is also in play: For instance, one chair is made of wood but has a core of injected polyurethane, to reduce weight. Trimarchi says that the company's far-reaching aesthetic is a well-known company attribute. So all graphic design work associated with the client must have that same panache.

Trimarchi designed the company's logo—a straightforward word mark—in 1999. It is simple and solid. At first glance, it might not seem to be an apt or at least highly stylish graphical representation of the core organization. But the art director had a very good reason for the basic nature of his design: If he chooses, he can use the letters in the word "Alias" almost like television screens through and around which he projects additional color, texture and/or graphics. The screens stay the same shape, but they constantly reveal new information about the client as it evolves and changes over time.

The identity for Alias, created by Fragile (of Milan), is like a clear container. Visual messaging of all sorts can be shown through, inside, and around the container. This keeps the identity changeable and fresh for the fashion-forward furniture manufacturer year after year.

Fragile also uses the client's actual products and product components in the same way: Their shapes can be containers for art or information, or they can be formed and reformed in patterning. They are ingredients, Trimarchi says: "It's like working in the kitchen. With the same basic ingredients, you can make cake or béchamel."

It's an approach that Fragile likes. For a recent logo design for Poste Italiane, the Italian postal service, Trimarchi created a system composed of photos of six different Italian landscapes. Each shot is underlined by a yellow, horizontal strip containing the logotype. The pictures can, in the future, be easily replaced with other photos or visual information, such as Italian architecture, famous artists or art, or different people, depending on the corporate mission as it develops over time.

"This is the post service," he explains, "but it is really Italy. If the company management changes and wants to alter the identity, they can change the software part of the design, but the hardware is fixed. If the management decides to get into banking in the future, there is no problem. They can change the identity, but it is still linked with the postal service."

The key, the designer says, is to tell a story that allows the client to accommodate the future and its eventual brand evolution. A static, moment-in-time logo doesn't work for clients anymore.

Trimarchi is quick to point out that the "ingredients" philosophy is not a fallback style for his company, but an approach that can be crafted in new and different ways for clients. "For any design, you know that the company and its market will not be the same over time. We try to leave a window open for them, windows to the future. The same car company whose customers want performance cars today may produce hybrid cars tomorrow. They don't want to covert themselves totally, but they need to be able to face new challenges," he says.

A designer should care for a client like an arborist cares for a tree, he says. The tree may be very large, but you need to care for it regularly—and that's much easier to do if there is an open and ongoing system in place.

But many clients are very accustomed to closed systems: In the past, a client would have received a static logo and a strict guidelines manual from his designer, and he would have been strongly encouraged to stick with both. Evolution is not a part of the plan. If the company changed enough, the designer would suggest a new or updated static logo: The old mark would be modified or thrown out.

"This is why our job is so difficult: Clients don't always understand this way. But we show them that it is better to have a process in place rather than a final solution. We don't give them a corporate design—we give them a corporate personality. Once upon a time, a person would be defined as 'elegant,' and that person acted that way all of the time. Today, people and companies are diverse. You can be elegant but make a range of choices in your life for your bike, your clothes, your car. A smart logo allows the company to emit its personality throughout its lifetime, no matter what it is at the time," he notes.

The evolution of Alias illustrates how a "living" system works. In 2003, the Alias logo was used in a new campaign for the company, suggesting that its furniture is "essential and light." On the cover of that year's catalog, a water bottle with the name Alias on it appeared. It represented purity, harmony in purpose, vocation, change, and flexibility.

"The water bottle is a commodity," Trimarchi notes, "but it is also an archetype: It has proven to be long-lasting in our lives." This is how Alias wished its new line to be seen: Yes, a chair is a commodity item, but a chair designed by Alias has timelessness, practicality, and purity of purpose.

Also part of the 2003 promotion was a series of pictures in the catalog that showed the most interesting design details of the products in order to highlight the extreme care on manufacturing process: The chair legs are represented as aluminum, artificial "bones," and every subtle curve of the armrest enter the pages with large close-up.

In 2004, Trimarchi took the ingredients one step further. His team assembled chairs from that year's collection in groupings or structures that, when photographed, accentuated their sculptural qualities. Alone, each chair is a work of high design. But when seen as a grouping, even great visual interest is achieved.

"Here, not just one chair forms an icon, like before. Now the whole family of products could be the icon. Imagine it like a company of dancers: The design and the beauty comes from the whole group," he says.

In that period, the strategy of the company was to present a family of products with the same design developed on different themes. For this reason, Fragile started to think to the most significant and original way to show the importance of the whole, single collection. The collection pictures were used on the initial pages of each chapter of the company catalog, in order to introduce the single pieces.

In 2006, the pictures taken for 2004 were repurposed. Mirrored and flipped, then repeated, new and intriguing patterns are formed. A new recipe is complete, but it contains the same ingredients as were used before.

"The multiplication by computer forms interesting wallpapers. I like the idea to create two-dimensional graphics through the use of three-dimensional items. We can continue to play with the basic elements, too—color, black-and-white, 2-D, 3-D. It all refreshes the brand but is always linked to the mood and expression of the product," Trimarchi says.

As part of the 2003 promotion for Alias, the Fragile designers isolated visually interesting parts from that year's lines and used them as illustrations in the catalog. Shown here is a piece from the back of a featured chair and the same piece shown as part of the assembled chair.

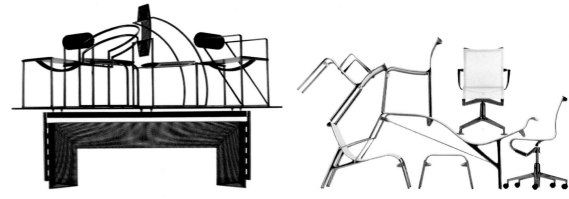

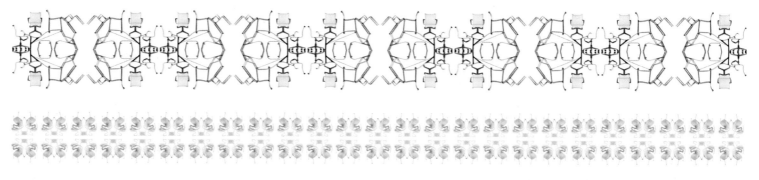

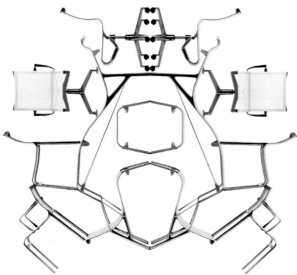

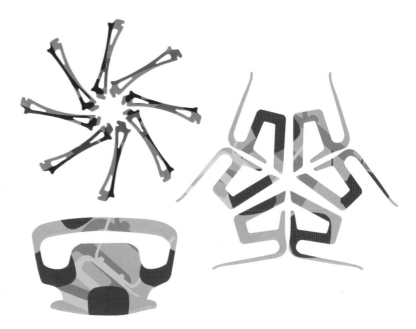

For the 2004 collections, creative director Mario Trimarchi took the "ingredients" approach one step further. He built structures using the furniture, highlighting their unique forms and sculptural qualities. He compares this approach to that of a dance company: Together, the group can create even more beauty.

In 2006, the pictures taken for 2004 were repurposed. Mirrored and flipped, then repeated over and over, new and intriguing patterns are formed. The same ingredients can be used to complete an entirely new and delicious recipe, Trimarchi says.

In 2008, the photos taken of individual furniture components were repurposed again. Recharged with vibrant color, the pieces are reassembled into intriguing patterns. They are like an entirely new alphabet. In Alias' first-ever retail store, which is completely white, the alphabet components provide the only color.

This invitation cover and trade show display show how the new patterns and wallpapers can be used.

The new patterns continued to move the identity forward by building up new icon-based visual alphabets, from the single piece to the family, and here from the family to an entire universe. The patterns covered many the surface, become wallpaper to be extended in all the directions, and were used for covering all the vertical walls of the stand at the Salone del Mobile Fair in Milan, on the invitation card, on the cover of the company profile, and in a certain number of internal pages of this document.

Then in 2008, Alias opened its first retail store in Milan, called AliasShop. The store is distributed over two floors. Interior space is extremely fresh and white, in order to emphasize the products without suggesting any idea of actual placement. The layout, designed by architect Renato Stauffacher (CEO of Alias), is aimed to express the company's key values: lightness, technology, and innovation. The products are shown in their white versions and are located in full-transparent glass cabinets. The only presence of color is the vibrant Fragile alphabet.

For this event and Alias' newest collection, this new alphabet was based on the silhouettes of furniture parts. These, the designer says, have as much beauty and are just as carefully designed as the furniture pieces.

"People can't usually see the individual pieces of a chair, but it is a reality and is perhaps more beautiful. Each piece is used like an icon, like a logo. In the catalog, we could use these pieces to form a flower or another shape and place it across the spread from the chair itself—show people the beauty of the technology alongside of the product," he explains.

The Alias identity system is one that will continue to evolve. A process rather than a static identity solution is a better fit for most companies, Trimarchi says. "We spend time with our client and develop a system that can live on—not a corporate identity, but a corporate personality."

Creative direction: Mario Trimarchi/Fragile
Graphic design: Mario Trimarchi with Andrea Plenter, Elena Riva/
Fragile team

Methis
Identity Design

Fragile, Milan, Italy

Methis, the office furniture division of the Coopsette Group (an Italian group that develops large building projects, from pre-fabricated structures to railway superstructures) has a particularly unique product: It offers clients stylish office furnishings with a twist. While most competitors provide predetermined, preset solutions for office layouts, Methis designs spaces especially for each customer's needs and wants. It believes that the work environment must revolve around the quality and varieties of relationships between people.

When Fragile was invited to create a new identity for Methis, the design team could immediately understand what the client wanted. Fragile designers like to create identities that are very responsive to their client's needs and the times. For Methis, they considered what sort of identity could indicate the client's human touch in their work while at the same time leaving the window open to change in the future.

"It is very interesting that in the field of office furniture and design, there are religions. Some people want to show their company as an organism. Some people want to show their office as a pyramid, or a skyscraper, or whatever. These are kinds of hierarchies that people believe in very much," explains Mario Trimarchi, principal of Fragile. Methis, by comparison, is concerned with human needs and relationships, not predetermined hierarchies.

A key component of the original Methis logo was a series of three shapes—a square and two rectangles—that are sized according to the golden ratio (the ratio of line lengths used produces a measurable mathematical sequence that has proven to be pleasing to the eye). The client wanted to keep the series but change the styling of the word mark.

This presented a special challenge to Fragile: How could both the old logo and the new word mark be updated in a coordinated manner that maintained the visual equity of the old mark?

Trimarchi explains. "Methis' spirit is to be partners with their clients. They are an elastic, flexible, transparent partner: They see their clients' point of view. They see everything about the quality of the clients' work and produce adaptable solutions. So we wanted to show transparency in their logo, with the human touch."

Trimarchi created an irregular hand-drawn scribble pattern, and then ran it inside of the shapes of the letters in "Methis" and in the original logo. The shapes are not completely filled, indicating process. The letters in Methis are also hand-drawn, further communicating the human touch in the client's work.

"We want to show that the human is at the center of their design, not technology—not perfection, but man with all of his imperfection," Trimarchi adds. "We have created this logo by hand, to put on focus the centrality of human being, just as the company creates its work putting the man on the center."

In the future, Trimarchi says that while the outline of the shapes and letters will remain the same, what fills them may change, according to the client's evolving personality and situation.

(Opposite) Methis, a company that works closely with customers to produce customized office furniture solutions, needed an identity that revealed its handcrafted approach to business. Fragile designers experimented with a word mark and logo filled with hand scratching.

(Left and below) Shown here is the final scratch pattern and Methis identity. The letters and logo are not completely filled in to suggest process, not prefab solutions.

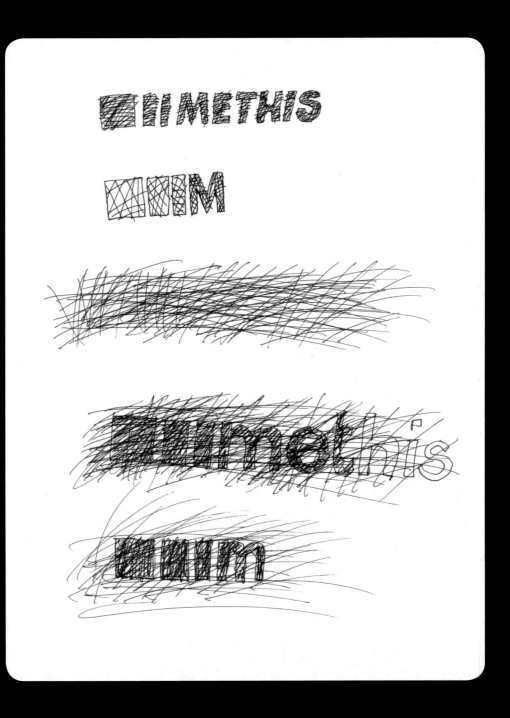

Design Firm	**Cato Purnell Partners**
Client	**Dubai Airport organization**
Project	**Corporate Identity Redesign**

Dubai Airports is redefining the phrase "world's biggest airport." It manages both of the major airports in Dubai, the already existing Dubai International Airport, as well as what will be an enormous new facility, Al Maktoum International at Dubai World Central, a global aviation hub covering 140 square kilometers (about 54 square miles). In a region where real estate, banking, and many other moneyed businesses are expanding at an unprecedented rate, Dubai Airports is truly becoming a global aviation center, fortuitously located near the geographic center of the world.

The Dubai Airport organization began working with Cato Purnell Partners in 2007 to develop an identity that would unite its holdings as well as identify Dubai as a new world hub. The new identity would be a complete departure from the previous one, which was no longer unique in the marketplace.

> For us, the Dubai airport project gave us a chance to look at local culture and reinterpret it.

"The Dubai region is an economic hotbed right now," says Graham Purnell, partner with Cato Purnell Partners, headquartered in Melbourne, Australia. "It's a rapidly emerging region with many large-scale projects. For us, the Dubai airport project gave us a chance to look at local culture and reinterpret it. It was a great mix of tradition and modernity."

Purnell notes that the rapid expansion of business in Dubai has attracted many designers and design firms there, but not all have succeeded. "You must be very careful of regional sensibilities. Arabic calligraphy, for instance, has wonderful forms to look at, but we can't read it. We have really good people in Dubai who work as our sounding board as we design. You need to work with local people to bring your ideas to light."

"We saw these airports as a true global hub, connecting people from all other parts of the world. Bringing that alive became our main direction," Purnell says.

The designers had a host of key words around which to build their work: global hub, where heritage meets the future, integration, connection, movement. A number of these concepts were explored, but the direction that eventually emerged struck the right chord and checked off every word on the list.

(Top) At the identity's launch, the new design posed a definite breakthrough in its freshness and energy.

(Center and bottom) In these images from a trade show, the fractal imaging introduced by the new identity is evident in the architecture and patterning. In the photo at left, moving kaleidoscopic images are projected onto an overhead screen.

Dubai Airports

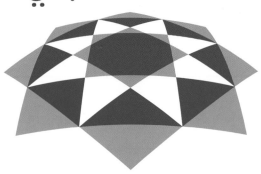

Dubai International

Dubai World Central
Al Maktoum International

The new logos for Dubai Airports, Dubai International, and Dubai World Central mark an enormous new air hub located at the geographic center of the world, Dubai. Created by Cato Purnell Partners, the new identity system mirrors mosaics from the region, while giving the ancient art form a new spin, through kaleidoscopic imagery.

The strongest direction emerged from local art: traditional patterning found on fabrics and formed in tile. Mosaics are an ancient art in the region, dating back to the seventh century: Unlike Byzantine mosaics, which form figurative representations such as pictures of religious figures, Islamic mosaics are mostly geometric and/or mathematical. But despite their rigorous patterning, Islamic mosaics feel alive with energy—an ancient yet perfect analogy for a modern airport.

The designers imagined the ceiling of a mosque, beautifully patterned and still visually relevant despite the passing of many hundreds of years. It is a familiar image and one could—despite its inherent visual interest and lovely color—be interpreted as cliché. Cato Purnell partner Ken Cato travels regularly in the region and has amassed a great knowledge of such arts. The mosaic inspiration felt appropriate and true.

"You have to take the familiar and re-evaluate it," says Purnell. "You have to breathe new life into things that other people might overlook."

To bring new life to the concept of the mosaic, Purnell's team literally turned it inside-out and let new light shine on it: They took a star-centered design from the inside, concave surface of a mosque dome and spherized it on the outside of a globe.

The mosaic star could serve as a strong unifying device, and it also graphically marks the centralized geographic position of the city on the globe. The star and patterning that grows out from it can be changed in color to identify separate holdings or operations. They could easily be animated into moving, kaleidoscopic images that change endlessly, sparking new interest in the eye of the viewer. Even in the static image, though, movement

More onscreen and LCD projections of the energetic imagery.

Dubai Airports

The image on this poster was created using a photo of a runway with planes sitting on it.

At the time this book was written, in late 2008, the new identity system was still being implemented. This shot shows how patterns and photos can be injected into the kaleidoscope. The possibilities for new visual information are endless, while the basic form remains the same and identifiable.

We were able to take traditional elements and make people look at them in a new context that is quite surprising. Working with a different culture is always a positive experience. We are always learning.

is directed in toward the center and away again, just as travelers move to and from the airport.

For Dubai International, a blue and gold color scheme was selected. The color scheme is derivative of the region, tweaked to give it a modern feel. Dubai World Central uses a quartet of blues.

Other sub-brands are easily accommodated by the new system. Additional patterning and colors are overlaid, but the strong tie to the center star remains. At this writing, the sub-brands are still in prerelease stage, but the family ties to central identities are strong.

The new system uses plenty of photography that centers on the connections people make, with each other and with other parts of the world. There is a definite sense of motion introduced through blurs, suggesting the energy of the airports.

A kaleidoscopic effect is extremely versatile. The theme allows flexibility in application, is symbolic of movement and energy, ties in with patterns of the region—it strongly resembles mosaics—and provides an opportunity to instantly recognize images as linked to Dubai Airports. Modern photography is spun into traditional patterning.

The typefaces were selected to deliver the best clarity. These logos need to be reproduced at varying sizes. As English is a second language for many people in the area, but it still needed to be clear, yet distinctive and ownable to Dubai Airports and project the professionalism of this organization, yet be complementary to all the sub-brands. The Arabic script that was specified comes in many versions and is exceptionally versatile, more so than English copy, allowing the Arabic to script to be developed after the English to make sure they would work together in dual language lockups.

Implementing the new identity across the vast expanse of the client's holdings is still under way. The sphere is being played out on everything from tarmacs, windows, and vehicles to uniforming, signage, and advertising.

Purnell says he is delighted with the project's outcome. "We were able to take traditional elements and make people look at them in a new context that is quite surprising," he says. "Working with a different culture is always a positive experience. We are always learning."

The culture and business is well represented through the new mark. "It gives a sense of character to the entire place. "The audiences for these airports are enormously broad," Purnell says. The new identity speaks to them all, residents and nonresidents alike, as they come and go.

The pieces of the logos themselves are also very versatile. Here, a moderate close-up, extreme close-up, and the insertion of photos provide new impressions of the same identity.

Pluna
Identity Design

Cato Purnell Partners, Melbourne, Australia

A client's very origins can be a great gift to a designer. Such was the case with Pluna, the national airlines of Uruguay. The small airline's previous identity was nationalistic and depleted from years of use. It said nothing informative about the country.

"Uruguay means 'river of painted birds,'" explains Graham Purnell, partner with Cato Purnell Partners, who undertook the identity redesign for the small airline. His team believed that the new identity could say a lot more about the natural beauty and intrigue of the place.

Partner Ken Cato undertook the project himself. He began by considering ways to represent the country through visuals that resonated with natural beauty. A literal river of colorful birds was an ideal direction, but it took plenty of tinkering to puzzle together an Escher-like design that also contained the birds and colors that were authentic to the country. Cato's team undertook extensive research efforts to figure out which birds would be appropriate, then spent hours harmonizing their forms and strong colors.

The lowercase lettering that forms the Pluna word mark is friendly, honest, and simple. This lettering provides a contrast against the bird pattern. It's plain and straightforward—very different from the exciting, busy bird pattern.

The final design looks progressive in speed and energy, and it is certainly more modern. Played out on aircraft, in interior airport applications, in overhead signage, magazine, and newspaper ad templates and more, it has been well received by the citizenry of Uruguay as well as abroad.

Purnell believes it appeals to citizens because they pick up on the river of painted birds, which gives a sense of national patriotism. It appeals to travelers as it gives a sense of festivity, excitement, and natural environment.

Cato Purnell created a vibrant new identity for Pluna Airlines, the national airline of Uruguay. The country's name means "river of painted birds," which is exactly what inspired the design.

"It was quite courageous for Pluna to go with the design. No one has done anything like that before—the colors, graphics, birds. Everyone does stripes and symbols, so this is revolutionary in the marketplace," says Purnell of the bold new identity. "The fact that they allowed us to print it on their aircraft in so many colors is remarkable. This identity offers a sense of diversity for a very colorful country."

Design Firm	**Chermayeff & Geismar**
Client	**Library of Congress**
Project	**Logo Design**

There are some logo solutions that just seem inevitable—not predictable, but somehow, just right. Chermayeff & Geismar's logo for the Library of Congress in 2008 is such a design. Once viewed, it's hard to imagine that any other solution would be possible.

Founded in 1800 to serve the research needs of the United States Congress, the Library of Congress is the nation's oldest federal cultural institution. It is an organization well known by name to citizens of the United States, but few people ever appreciate the true extent of its wingspan. The largest library in the world, it contains millions of books, recordings, photographs, maps, and manuscripts in its collections, and millions more are added every year.

> We wanted to convey the idea of a very lively place, at the forefront of things. It is definitely not just a tomb for books.

Additionally, the Library of Congress includes the research arm of Congress; the U.S. Copyright Office; the American Folklife Center; an extensive Braille library and resource center; the Kluge Center, which rewards lifetime achievement in the humanities; the Law Library of Congress, which contains the world's largest collection of law books and legal resources; an extensive poetry and literature center; and millions of film, video, and sound recordings. More than 5,000 people work to support the Library's efforts.

The Library's sheer scale, however, proved to be a liability when it came to its identity. Like many large organizations, various divisions had developed their own logos and graphics over time, and there were a handful of differing marks in circulation for the Library itself, with little attempt at coordination. So while most citizens and members of Congress knew about the Library, few recognized its scope and reach.

As a result, in mid-2006, the Library embarked on an overall branding study to bring greater cohesiveness and integration to the Library's communications and overall identity. Developed by the Library's Brand Working Group and Fleishman-Hillard, the study defined a clear vision statement and a comprehensive brand message architecture. It left open the next step, the development of a unified graphic identity to ensure "thinking, communicating and behaving as one enterprise connected by a unified vision."

The new identity system created by Chermayeff & Geismar for the Library of Congress includes a logo that is completely ownable by the Library. Incorporating the images of a book and a flag, it's an ideal image for America's library.

Various mock-ups of the new logo.

It was at this point in mid-2007 that Chermayeff & Geismar was retained by the Library of Congress to develop a new visual identity program that would complement the overall branding initiative and better represent the complex, modern institution the Library of Congress had become.

Tom Geismar was quite familiar with the Library. He had designed a series of major exhibitions and related graphics over the past decade and was concurrently heavily involved in helping to develop a new, more interactive visitor experience, a new wayfinding system, and so on. To begin the project, Geismar conducted a series of interviews with a dozen senior people representative of the key constituents of the Library. Many of the interviewees were familiar with the issues, having served for many months on the Library's Brand Working Group. Jo Anne Jenkins, the chief operating officer, was a key member of this group.

Chermayeff & Geismar also conducted an extensive visual audit of materials produced by the various divisions and programs. "The audit yielded many different identities and a wide variety of graphic styles. That's part of the problem," says Chermayeff & Geismar partner Sagi Haviv.

Chermayeff & Geismar felt that the new identity needed to unite all the pieces, to bring everyone under the same banner. The task was to find a logo that graphically represents not only the Library and its contents, but its aspirations and future as well.

Creating a new identity for such an iconic institution with so many layers and so much history is a challenge, Geismar acknowledges. "It contains books, but like all large libraries, it is rapidly digitizing its collection. We wanted to convey the idea of a very lively place, at the forefront of things. It is definitely not just a tomb for books."

Previous logos had focused on the dome of the Library's most famous building, the magnificent Thomas Jefferson Building, an iconic structure that, in truth, presents the picture that springs to mind for most people when they think of the Library of Congress. "But we felt that the dome as an image is quite static, and perhaps suggests the past more than the future," notes Haviv.

"In any case," as Geismar explains," the Jefferson Building is right across the street from the U.S. Capitol, whose dome is considerably larger and certainly more famous and more recognizable in the Washington landscape. We see it on the news every evening."

As visual explorations were initiated, Ivan Chermayeff, Geismar, and Haviv all began to develop different concepts for how best to symbolize this complex institution.

One source of inspiration was the Thomas Jefferson Building itself. Completed in the 1890s and fully restored in the 1990s, the building is filled with elaborate artwork, murals, sculptures, and decorative patterns. Much of the art focuses on symbolic themes relevant to a great cultural institution. One image found throughout the building (and on the top of its dome) is that of a torch or flame, symbolizing knowledge and enlightenment or learning.

"We developed a number of torch-inspired ideas. It was one of the ideas mentioned by a number of members of the Library staff, and in terms of meaning it seemed very appropriate," notes Geismar. "But while some torch concepts made it to the final rounds, in the end we recognized that it was very difficult to make a torch or flame that is sufficiently distinct and memorable. There are just too many of them out there."

These early sketches reveal how the design of the logo emerged. Other concepts, including torches (to represent the light of learning and the torch atop the Library's dome) were also explored.

The inspiration for the lettering in the system was inspired by the incised inscription over the entrance to the Library's Great Hall. The classic Roman style was very similar to Trajan, which was the face eventually chosen.

The Library is an enormous organization with many branches. So it was natural that, over the years, various identities and design approaches had emerged.

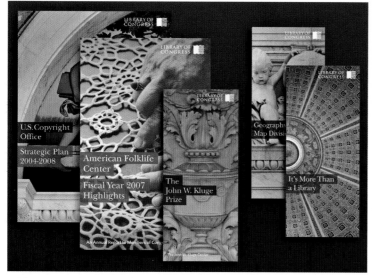

This collection of brochures that use the new identity shows how the many different Library branches could be coordinated, yet through the use of the organization's rich photographic and art resources, be kept fresh and unique.

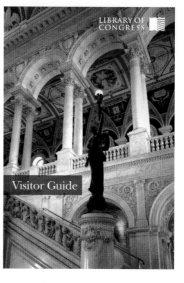

A selection of Library resources with the new identity in place.

The new logo has distinct animation possibilities, as shown by these stills.

As Haviv points out, "Just do a Google image search for 'torch logo' and thousands of examples come up."

Another obvious direction was to convey the concept of a book or group of books. A number of these were studied, and some interesting designs emerged. The challenge here was to develop an image that somehow conveyed more than just books, one that could also be viewed as aspirational.

A design created by Haviv that held special resonance all the way through the sketching and presentation processes was a book that essentially took the form of a waving flag. It proved to be the perfect combination and was the mark eventually recommended by Chermayeff & Geismar.

"A national library needs something really unique. Who can claim the American flag more than the national library? This solution was specific to them: No one else could have this mark," Haviv says.

Symbolically, the new logo speaks of knowledge and information flowing from a central core. It suggests life and motion through its wave. Its stripes suggest the wide array of services that are available through the library.

Another key element of the new identity is the way that the Library's name is depicted. In the initial interviews, Geismar discovered that the word *The,* while always included in prior identities, was not actually part of the Library's legal name. Eliminating *The* made possible the creation of a much more symmetrical word mark that can easily be used to the left or right of the symbol, or below it, stacked in two lines or played out in one, without losing easy recognition.

One inspiration for the lettering was the incised inscription over the entrance to the Library's Great Hall. Reading "Library of Congress," the letters are in a classic Roman style, similar to the typeface Trajan. Trajan, in turn, is styled after the classic inscriptions on Rome's Trajan Column, which some

historians believe marked the location of the two great libraries of Rome. So the choice of Trajan—which evokes a sense of dignity and tradition—was an easy one.

As part of their recommendations, Chermayeff & Geismar also developed an approach to the design of brochures and reports, which in the past have been completely uncoordinated. One part of the recommendation is to feature photography of the artwork found in the Jefferson Building. Produced by more than fifty American artists, sculptors, and craftsmen, it provides a rich trove of imagery, and one can almost always find an appropriate representation. Other parts of the recommendation were the use of full color; the adoption of Baskerville as the typeface for titles; and the inclusion of the Library's graphic identity on the cover of all pieces.

The overall graphic identity study lasted approximately six months. During this time, Geismar made two interim presentations to the Library's Brand Working Group. After each presentation, refinements and revisions were made. Then, in December 2007, a final presentation and recommendation was made to the Group and to Dr. James Billington, the Librarian of Congress.

For Chermayeff & Geismar, the project was a major one. The successful outcome was to some extent a validation of the firm's approach of working closely together to find the best possible result for each client. Notes Haviv, "There is no ego here—we all help each other find the best quality for every client. When we all come into the project, the work quickly gets better."

(As of this writing, Chermayeff & Geismar was starting to develop guidelines for the implementation of the graphic identity.)

Principal design credit: Tom Geismar and Sagi Haviv

Armani Exchange
Identity Design

Chermayeff & Geismar, New York, New York

Armani Exchange has a well-known mark in fashion-conscious circles, but the original logo's visual strength on labels, marketing materials, and particularly in advertising was not as robust as it could be—especially for a brand that was inspired by military exchange store merchandise.

The mark was simply two letters—*A* and *X*—separated by a thin line. The letters were set in a reworked Bodoni, but the original beauty of the font's thicks and thins were changed until the letterforms no longer felt substantial. The entire design simply felt squeezed and lightweight.

Armani's creative directors brought in Chermayeff & Geismar to evaluate the design.

"The typeface used in the original symbol was a text face, which, unlike display faces, is not meant to be viewed at large sizes. The letters needed to feel like they went together," explains Sagi Haviv, a partner and designer with Chermayeff & Geismar. "We also wanted to make the combination wider so that they could fit 'Armani Exchange' underneath."

The designers' solution was simple but ingenious: They redrew the letterforms based on the classic font Didot, which is already used for the rest of the Armani brand family. The bold strokes in the letters were made parallel. This produced a more unified look, but

Old logo design

Armani Exchange's original logo had, over time, begun to look squeezed and insubstantial. It did not reproduce well on top of busy backgrounds—including fashion photography.

the letters were still light, and although elegant, appeared too weak and lacking visual impact. The solution was to reverse each letter out of an identically sized black box.

The small gap between the boxes neatly replaces—in reverse—the original thin line in the old design. The effect is definitely stronger, and the design survives better at smaller sizes. An additional benefit: The two boxes look like dog tags, perfect for a brand with a military foundation.

"Now you have a bold mark. It has more bulk, more meat," Haviv says. "It will stand out on busy photos. This was not an approach that the client anticipated. They thought we were going to reinvent the 'A|X'— or just place it in a shape. We ended up integrating the two approaches and produced a bold, modern, and fashionable mark that retains the brand equity of the original."

The Chermayeff &Geismar designers also developed a series of four icons that can be used as brand identifiers. The designs were based on forms produced by the letters *A* and *X*, on the shape of eagles' wings, and on sergeant's stripes, another reference to the brand's origins.

New logo design

Chermayeff & Geismar created an elegantly simple solution for Armani: It reworked the letters, then placed them in boxes, which easily gives the logo more weight and presence, as shown on this billboard.

The C&G designers also created a series of four icons that can be used as brand identifiers. As this sample shows, all were based on the shapes of the letters A and X.

Design Firm	**Mattson Creative**
Client	**Grace Cathedral, San Francisco**
Project	**Logo Design**

GRACE
CATHEDRAL

What is a church? Is it simply an organization? A building? A shelter or concept?

These are questions that church organizers wrestle with all of the time. For the staff of Grace Cathedral, a 100-year-old Gothic cathedral that sits, solemn and imposing, on San Francisco's landmark Nob Hill, the answers were not exactly what they wanted. The building itself is a magnificent city icon, but its historic architecture did not exactly present a welcoming face. In fact, the structure presented just the sort of scowly, stiff, somehow judgmental face that many city residents moved to San Francisco to escape.

> ## The church wanted to represent its open-door policy and how it reaches out to the community.

But behind the cathedral doors, the picture is much different. The church is progressive and active in the city community. Its staff works hard to involve all peoples and to create a place of discussion. In short, they want to change the paradigm of what a church is: not a fortress, but a comfortable haven where all are welcome and nurtured.

Still, there's the issue of the actual architecture—beautiful, but potentially off-putting. Even the church's centenarian status carried some stodgy baggage: How relevant could a 100-year-old church be?

But the celebration of the landmark's anniversary and the press it would generate also offered the opportunity for a positive change in direction. Church organizers decided that a contemporary anniversary logo, one that could have life after the actual event, might help people better understand that the organization is a living organism, not a museum.

"It's not just a castle," says Ty Mattson of Mattson Creative. He became involved with the project through the now-defunct firm Templin Brink. Mattson was intrigued with how the identity project bridged faith and culture. The church did have an existing logo—a modern representation of a Gothic cathedral—but Mattson describes it as menacing. "It was the kind of mark that had all of the stigma of a closed-door sort of church. Which is not what they desired to communicate. They wanted to represent their open-door policy and how they reach out to the community. The new logo

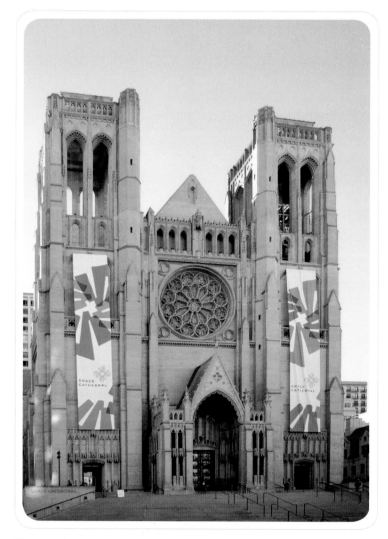

The new logo and identity that Mattson Creative developed for Grace Cathedral in San Francisco delivers a progressive, welcoming message that the building's architecture might not. While the landmark might be imposing, the church's organizers wanted everyone to know that it is a friendly, caring place.

GRACE CATHEDRAL   GRACE CATHEDRAL

GRACE CATHEDRAL   GRACE CATHEDRAL   GRACE CATHEDRAL

This asterisk-like design was part of the first round of Mattson's presentation to clients, and it made it all the way to the end. It presents the idea of being on a hill and being a light to the community. It has a celebratory sense, and also includes a cross. It's an eye-catching design in black and white, one that would really come to life in color. The designer points out how the individual pieces are imperfect. "Imperfection is a nice theme when it comes to church logos," Mattson says. "Perfection is not a church value. Irregularity is welcome. This felt very hand-done—nothing is perfect."

The client had asked that the designer work in the notion that the church is open to all in the community. Here, he experiments with a walkway that leads to the doors of the church. Playful line work demonstrates the doors' accessibility. Ultimately, this exploration felt too whimsical and playful. The literal depiction lacked the significance of the more abstracted symbols.

GRACE CATHEDRAL   GRACE CATHEDRAL

GRACE CATHEDRAL   GRACE CATHEDRAL

GRACE CATHEDRAL

GRACE CATHEDRAL   GRACE CATHEDRAL

Here Mattson brought in a common symbol, the dove, but transformed it to make it look more like an angel. "There's imperfection in this design," he says, "as if it's hand-drawn."

The designer liked this design, but the client felt it was too corporate. "I like the interaction, the idea of the three components in the trinity. It felt cohesive to me, but it was a little too space-age for them."

GRACE CATHEDRAL

GRACE CATHEDRAL

Mattson felt this design was too "expected" and a little Olympic. The idea behind the concept was community and acceptance, an extremely important message for the large alternative lifestyle population in the San Francisco area. "This is an involving design, one that causes the viewer to look at it longer," he says.

This design had a celebratory nature that Mattson also liked. In an abstract sense, the shapes can be viewed as people. That sense of abstraction could be continued on in how people view the church, not as an object of architecture but as an organic being.

GRACE CATHEDRAL

A play on the shape of a dove, this design introduces the idea of prayer, of the uplifted hand in worship, or even the idea of offering service to the community. Mattson maintains the hand-drawn feel to the design.

This last-minute addition to Mattson's presentation to the client made it to final consideration. The trio of simple, interlocking rings just felt right to him, and the client liked it, too. "What the client responded to, I think, was the idea of imperfection," he says.

The client was most interested in Mattson's asterisk designs. It was simple, but worked on a number of levels. It incorporates the shape of a cross, certainly the central symbol of Christian faith, but in a subtle way. The mark also has an urban sensibility: The overlapping lines imply a city skyline, which represents Grace Cathedral's unique location. "Most importantly, I think this mark, more than any of the others, really conveys a sense of joy, which was missing from the previous visual language," says Mattson. "When someone experiences true 'grace' in their life, it's really an incredible thing. There is great joy in it, and I think this symbol evokes that in a way."

The Grace Cathedral identity played out in everyday applications.

needed to have an urban feel and it didn't necessarily have to integrate all of the traditional elements of Christianity."

Whatever he created had to be contemporary and relevant to the liberal, design-savvy San Francisco community. The new logo needed to define the church's name: What is grace?

One of the best ways to define the church was to re-examine its history and all of the good it has done over the years. "It's where people went when World War II ended to pray and celebrate. Martin Luther King spoke here, as did many contemporary leaders. People had come here to celebrate occasions like these for years. It's really a very significant place both culturally and spiritually," the designer explains. "The new mark needed to recognize that history, but more importantly it needed to convey their relevance and vision for the next 100 years. It's not meant to be commemorative. A good logo or brand doesn't just say who you were: It also explains who you will become next."

As he further developed the burst or asterisk concept, the designer explored making the shape less perfectly centered or mathematically divided. It gives the mark visual interest and brought forth the idea that being imperfect is perfectly acceptable.

For color, he suggested a light and dark green. It had a certain vibrancy to it, especially when compared to the flat gray stone of the church building.

"In church imagery," Mattson points out, "there is always plenty of red and other deep, rich colors. This goes in the opposite direction."

The type that accompanied the design had to be almost invisible, the designer says. "It's see-through, like a foundation. With a mark that is so expressive, there is no room for expression in the type. There cannot be any different sizes of type of initial caps or anything else. In the final design, the type is simply a foundation for the logo."

Sometimes a single client is actually composed of two partners with very different and forceful personalities. It can be a real problem for a designer. But sometimes, it's an absolute gift.

The latter was the case for Ty Mattson when he began working with a condo and apartment development company in Reno, Nevada. At the time, the client—then named Pacific West—had an abstract mountain logo. Its founders wanted an image overhaul, complete with new name, that better reflected the company's progressive values.

"From a personality standpoint, both partners in the company are mavericks. But they have different personalities and are not at all like other home builders. One partner is all about efficiency and being innovative when it comes to effectively building a community. The other partner is very creative and in charge of all of the marketing and is passionate about design innovation. Both are really into the environment and how their work will impact and improve people's lives. Their goal is to help people live closer to their work so they can spend more time with family, be home more, and reduce their environmental impact," Mattson says.

To better express their approach to life and home building, the partners came up with the name "The Collective." It was an emblematic name, rife with boldness and community. Mattson got to work.

He produced plenty of designs, but the design that was eventually chosen definitely challenged and excited the client the most. The word mark, adorned with what can be seen as ribbons blown

The logo and identity that Ty Mattson created for The Collective well represents both partners in the home development—the streamers represent the more creative, visionary partner, while the solid typography represents the more practical partner.

upward, had a sense of energy and inspiration that both partners and the designer liked.

"The design reads up, like celebratory streamers or flames. But it also reads down, like life getting organized and nestled into a home. In one sense, it communicates a reduction—the simplicity of living in a more efficient environment. On the other hand, it also communicates a celebration of life, organic and unplanned," says Mattson of the exuberant design.

The brand has wild colors, but the word mark portion of the logo is more restrained. "This represents the more conservative partner, who strives to build efficient homes. Both partners are equally passionate, and both partners' ideals are represented here."

Mattson originally imagined the design to be static, but soon saw animation possibilities. It was a logical next step to make the streamers wave on a website. (At this writing, the client had not fully implemented the wave, but it can be viewed at www.mattsoncreative.com/#collective.)

"Some people see the mark as a flame or like a celebratory explosion of streamers. Other people see it as life getting simplified and in order," says Mattson. Both definitions work, conceptually and philosophically, for the client.

THE COLLECTIVE

the collective

the collective

THE COLLECTIVE

THE COLLECTIVE

the collective

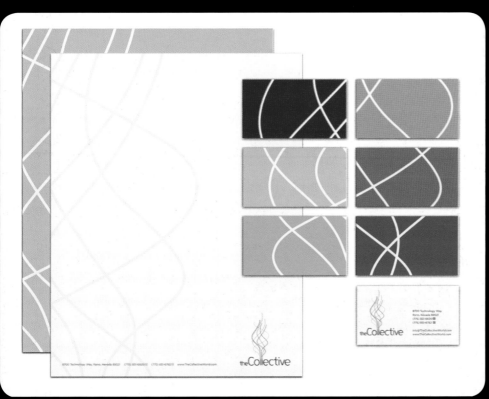

(Top) A selection of other logo ideas that Mattson created for the project.

(Center) The Collective's stationery system uses the streamers as intriguing art.

(Bottom) These proposed designs— coasters and direct mailers—show how the colors and art can be played out.

Design Firm	Moving Brands
Client	Swisscom, Switzerland
Project	Identity Design

Moving graphic identifiers are nothing new. They have existed in the world of television for years. However, considering a moving identity as a part of the very core of your brand is a more recent development.

Moving Brands, a London digital and branding agency, has the creation of a moving identity in the heart of its creative process. Movement is seen as an aspect of identity that can be ownable and distinctive for the brand, just like logo, colors or typeface. However, Moving Brands does not believe that every brand should be dynamic, no more so than every logo should be red or round or set in Times Roman.

In fact, just as a simple black-and-white monochrome version of the logo is created as a standard practice, they believe that a static logo needs to

> We realized that most of the agencies were not addressing the onscreen behavior of a brand. Often the thought was put into how a logo might live on the screen only afterwards.

be created for every dynamic identity. The possibility of it being dynamic, however, is an integral part of the creative process, and not simply an afterthought.

When Moving Brands was founded in 1998, its team was often asked to help larger design firms bring formerly static logos to life, explains founder Guy Wolstenholme.

"We realized that most of the agencies were not addressing the onscreen behavior of a brand. Often the thought was put into how a logo might live on the screen only afterwards," he says.

If a logo design is to be relevant today, it must work across all platforms, he adds, noting, "We feel this approach is truer to what clients need today." Logos today have both visual and behavioral characteristics, and some have sonic (or sound) identities as well. As the idea of multisensorial branding develops, touch and even smell will become increasingly important.

"You can express more about the brand through motion," says Darren Bowles, senior designer. A brand is like a person: If you only see a snapshot of the individual, you really learn very little about him. Motion helps convey personality through a series of behavior-filled moments.

The new Swisscom brand mark, created by Moving Brands (London), is intriguing in its static form as well as in its dynamic form, called the "life-form." The moving logo can be viewed at http://en.swisscom.ch.

The previous Swisscom logo no longer represented the company well in its modern focus on providing a very human, customized experience for its customers.

An early life-form sketch, which expresses its flowing form.

A sketch of the life-form, rotating around a clear axis.

A sketch of the life-form from a Moving Brands sketchbook.

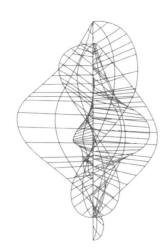

A moment in time from the life-form animation, showing the 3-D wire frame with full color.

The Moving Brand team is shown here in a "Brand Narrative" workshop, where participants sketch, in real time, to visualize client stories.

Bowles offers a caution regarding dynamic logos. "The level of expression through movement is key. Dynamic identities fail when the movement takes precedence over the story at the heart of the brand. The brand should be recognized for what it stands for, not just for how it moves."

The new identity that Moving Brands created for Swisscom is an excellent example of a brand that was designed to live across screen, print, and digital media. By its very footing in digital technology, Swisscom was the perfect client for a dynamic identity.

Swisscom is a leading telecommunications provider in Switzerland with a strong focus on IT services, media, and entertainment sectors. The new identity was created as a part of the client's consolidation of its various business divisions under one brand in order to make its customers' experiences with its services friendlier and easier to understand.

"For this brand to live and grow in the new media environment, it had to be more dynamic. It needed to offer much more expression," says Hanna Laikko, senior client lead for the Swisscom project.

A multisensorial identity must be considered from every angle, not just in terms of how it looks, but also how it might behave. "If you could touch it, how would it feel? If you dropped it, what would it do? If you could hear it, how would it sound?" says Bowles. "We talk about brands in a behavioral sense so that they will become easier to relate to."

The core story of the brand is completed together with the client. This is crucial, says Wolstenholme, because no one knows the story better. "The workshops we conduct with clients are very open and co-creative. They provide plenty of insights that inform the creative work. We often translate the stories real-time into sketches of form, shape, movement, and interaction."

With these core stories, emotions, and behavior drivers in hand, design could begin.

The former Swisscom logo was rooted in telecommunications and information technology. It represented what might be seen as blips of information going down the line. But Swisscom was transforming to be much more

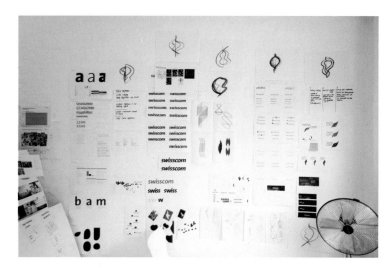

Shot on the studio wall of Moving Brands, this is the first brand mark that was signed off by the client.

Brand mark and word mark crafting materials from a creative review meeting in the Moving Brands' studio.

One of the beauties of the new Swisscom mark is its ability to be cropped into a healthy range of brand assets.

The flexibility of the new system is demonstrated in this range of other materials.

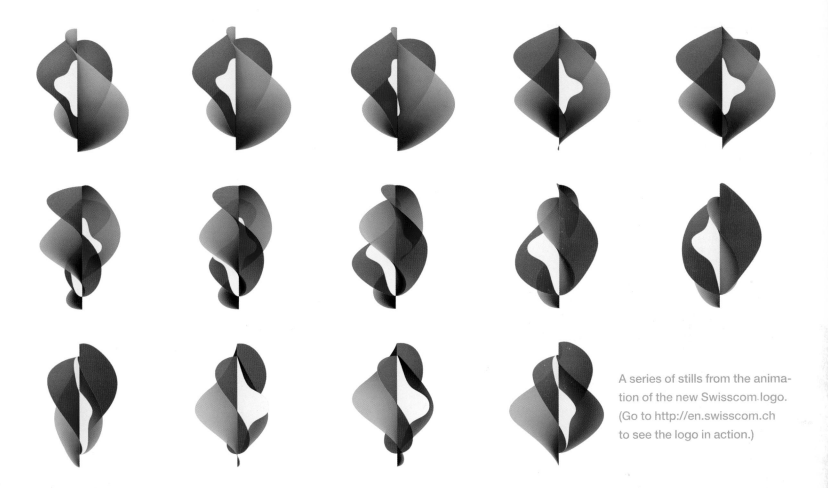

A series of stills from the animation of the new Swisscom logo. (Go to http://en.swisscom.ch to see the logo in action.)

about relationships and providing warm, welcoming, easy service that puts customers in focus. So there was a need for a new identity that could convey the change and engage the customers with the new Swisscom. However, there was also the need to retain the strong heritage of the well-trusted market leader.

For example, the colors blue and red are retained from the former identity. Swisscom also had a very recognizable pre-existing sonic identity.

The challenge was that the existing sonic identity was hard and technical. "It reflected the brand as it used to be," explains Laikko. "By using a female voice to hum the melody we introduced a human element that helped portray warmth, simplicity, and closeness to the recognizable sonic structure," says Wolstenholme.

The creative exploration involved discovering the main behavior drivers for static, moving, sonic, and responsive expressions of the brand. Live sketching and mood-mapping were utilized to gather criteria for the emotions and final behavior drivers. The client was engaged on the journey as much as possible through workshops and ongoing dialog. This enabled the creative team to quickly focus the development on the final route.

The final dynamic brand mark is a representation of the new Swisscom. It is designed to give Swisscom a broader meaning beyond Swiss-communication to Swiss-community. The symbol itself is called the "life-form." Its free-flowing planes reflect Swisscom's multilayered customer offering, pivoting around a single axis. They bring warmth, life, and emotion to the brand mark. The axis symbolizes Swisscom's heritage as a trusted national provider of smart technology.

"Swisscom has always been trusted as a company amongst the Swiss: That's the solid, rational axis at the center of the design," says Bowles. "But the company wanted to also be more emotive. The life-form's malleable layers show that Swisscom is adaptive and progressive."

The Swisscom word mark was designed in collaboration with Bruno Maag, a Swiss-origin typographer, at Dalton Maag. Still loosely based on the brand typeface Thesis, the word mark was redrawn to reflect the more personable, friendly Swisscom. The curves of the word marks' characters were crafted to complement the curves of the life-form.

Swisscom's red-and-blue color palette was refreshed and consolidated across the business lines. The role of white has been emphasized to bring a sense of space, clarity, and fresh innovation. More vibrant accent colors were added for expressiveness and silver to communicate premium offering.

How do the customers understand and appreciate the new design?

"The new Swisscom is more inclusive. We believe the new brand engages the customers by inspiring discussion and allowing people to have their own opinions about it," says Bowles. "The general perception is that it's a more friendly mark."

Identity Redesign

Moving Brands, London, England

Norton & Sons is a more than 185-year-old Savile Row tailor with a reputation for forward-looking, understated elegance, and flamboyance. It is the tailor of choice for largely independently wealthy, busy men who expect expert, "bespoke" sporting clothing made with the finest English materials—that is they create garments from scratch, specific to the customer. It is a decidedly behind-the-scenes, clubby place where no attention to detail is too small. It is so exclusive, it is said to produce only about 200 suits in a year, all hand-cut and hand-sewn.

"Walking into the shop, you do feel you are going somewhere special that is normally a closed world," explains Mat Heinl, design director at Moving Brands in charge of the Norton's identity redesign project. He worked with Moving Brands creative director and founder of Moving Brands Ben Wolstenholme. "There are lots of unwritten rules about how you do and don't promote yourself for business in Savile Row. Talking about money is just not the right thing to do."

Because of its firmly established reputation and traditions, the client's request for a new identity presented somewhat of a daunting puzzle, Heinl says. The shop's clients are older gentlemen, and nothing could be done that would possibly alienate them. But Norton's owner wanted to attract a younger client base as well.

The tailor's original identity had a more traditional, country feel, heavy burgundy, and deep green with gold lettering. Paper choices were all over the map, and the client's website had a different design altogether. The identity appeared to have developed organically and in places suffered from a sense of forced traditionalism. The true, deep tradition of the brand was missing.

"We have focused on what journey the company is on. That is what provides the script by which to make design decisions," Heinl explains. "It is possible to do something very of the moment, but in Savile Row, it is not about being radical. A lord who is coming in today and has for twenty years should [upon seeing a new identity] still think that the place is up to scratch—and a younger client would feel the same."

Wolstenholme, Heinl, and their team decided to build on the tradition. Sifting through boxes of old store records and advertisements for inspiration, they discovered a treasure trove—receipts from Winston Churchill, orders from dukes, and most important for the project at hand, an old word mark that they fell for immediately. Its letterforms felt sewn or possibly carved from wood. It could definitely be the basis for a new identity.

The first *S* in "Sons" is clearly upside down. The mistake had existed for many years on the shop front, perhaps the result of a long-ago repairman or by someone who knew no better. It was clear that the topsy letter had to stay upended in the new identity, which used all of the same basic letterforms spaced a bit tighter. The *S* added a quirky element that matched the business well.

A warrant—or seal of approval—long ago awarded by the Prussian royal family provided an appropriate "logo." (The use of a warrant is an unspoken but approved method of self-promotion in Savile Row.) The designers simplified the mark a bit for better reproduction.

The new identity is a perfect fit. "If you look at a shirt made by the tailor, it is not perfectly symmetrical. These shirts are personalized

NORTON & SONS

ESTD. 1821.

The new identity is redolent of the tailor's original, quirky signage—complete with upside-down S—yet it feels bold and new. Rich colors, papers, and foils speak clearly of the shop's roots, but the layout is modern. (Photos by Adam Laycock and Rex McWhirter.)

Above left, center and right: The fitting sheets, measures tickets, and other printed materials used behind the scenes have a very different color scheme, inspired by the rakish fabric colors sometimes used to line customers' clothing.

Above right and opposite: The use of black gray, and foils offer the elegant , staid part of the identity.

(Photos by Adam Laycock and Jack Laurance.)

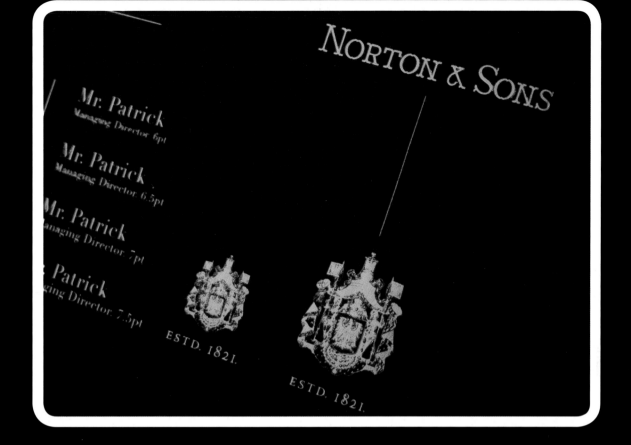

for you. They are perfect for the context of the wearer," Heinl says. The word mark and warrant were perfect for the context of Norton & Sons.

In some printed applications of the new identity, a long vertical line connects the word mark with the warrant. The line represents a chandelier that hangs in and is so emblematic of the store. The lockup of the word mark, "thread," and warrant was also inspired by beckets, which is part of the structure used to attach medals to uniforms.

Other elements of the identity that are seen by customers also speak of high quality and attention to detail—classic typefaces such as Caslon, Jensen, and British Rail; elegant foils; and lovely, thick papers in classic grays and blacks.

There is another part of the identity—an internal system of products—that is sometimes only seen by the Norton's staff but which is just as important. It includes measurement forms, order tickets, and garment labels called "buggy tickets." These tickets include space for cloth details, the date of creation, and handwritten signature of the cutter and tailor.

The internal and external systems were inspired by the two sides that each garment the tailor produces has: the outer side, which is clean and perfect, and the inner, structural layer.

"We wanted to match the quality of cloth and bespoke detailing of the outer layer, which is why we printed the stationery on fine papers with beautiful foil detailing. The inner layer is directly inspired by the more hidden parts of the garments. These are often very complicated, made of several different patterns or 'blocks' pieced together. The paper forms and labels take on that feel," Heinl explains. Some are printed in bright pink, blue, and yellow, a nod toward the flamboyant silks often ordered to line jackets for Norton & Sons clients.

Reaction to the new identity has been appropriately understated, and in some cases, completely absent—in other words, the perfect solution for the client.

"As for the customers, the older generation think of it as smart but don't really worry about it all too much. But the new identity has brought many younger guys into the fold," says Heinl. "It is a little bit special and quirky, but still classically correct."

Design Firm	Origin Communications
Client	Al Ahli Bank of Kuwait (ABK)
Project	Corporate Identity Redesign

Al Ahli Bank of Kuwait (ABK) is one of the Arabian Gulf's most established banking institutions with eighteen retail branches in Kuwait and an overseas branch in the UAE. The bank has a successful history serving public and private investors since its creation in 1967. When the bank's management decided it was time for an identity renewal, it was clear that the challenge would be balancing the bank's history with its modern vision for the future in a region where tradition equals trust for many customers.

The bank selected Origin Communications based in Dubai to undertake the project. "Origin's success stems from over fifteen years of working in the Arabian Gulf, accumulating vast regional experience in a constantly evolving market," explains Origin design director Trevor Halton. "Our team is made up of many nationalities including a number of Arabic staff, and we deal with consultants in many Middle Eastern countries."

> The bank is expanding around the region into markets where it is not yet established. To attract new accounts, they needed a fresher brand to compete in a dynamic market.

"We wanted to refresh the existing brand but were aware that we had to keep a link to the existing identity. Customer loyalty could erode with a drastic change. With a rapidly growing populace in the country, we wanted to create a more youthful image. Sixty percent of Kuwaitis are in their upper twenties. This changing demographic is having a real influence on branding in the country," notes Halton. "The bank is expanding around the region into markets where it is not yet established. To attract new accounts, they needed a fresher brand to compete in a dynamic market."

The bank's original logo had been in place for five years. The icon is believed to have been based on a symbol derived from a Persian coin. Its shape was quite complex. It was clear that a cleaner icon could strengthen its visual impact from a distance. The Latin letter portion of the old logo was set in a font probably meant to match the accompanying Arabic calligraphy, but its readability was not ideal. The colors used in the logo were also re-evaluated.

The new identity for ABK (Al Ahli Bank of Kuwait) is modern and corporate, yet it is based on a pattern found in a Persian mosaic. The design, created by Origin Communications, has some resemblance to the bank's previous design but has more "shelf presence."

ABK's original identity did not have a warm, modern feel that the bank desired. The color palette was drab, and many competitors also used blue. The use of all capital letters was neither friendly nor especially readable.

These sketches show the evolution the new design experienced. The interlocking lines were an appropriate metaphor for the client, who works with many different sorts of clients and individuals.

At the beginning of the project, the bank intended to refresh its logo, but as the project evolved, the design team at Origin realized that a full brand refreshment would be advisable. The client agreed.

A principal task was to sharpen the typography, as the English needed strengthening. To increase the impact, the Origin designers blended the lowercase a with an uppercase BK, to make the word mark unique. They then adjusted the a to give a graphic flow into the B. The serif of the K was curved to help it fit comfortably next to the B. This gave the bank a memorable word mark.

The Arabic lettering needed additional outside help. Arabic calligraphy is a specialized skill, says Halton, so for the past eight years Origin has worked with a Bahraini calligrapher who uses pen and ink to create letterforms that are not only readable, but also stylistically appropriate for the project.

"Initially, we had made recommendations to replace the calligraphy with a modern Arabic font, but the client requested that we preserve this part of the original logo. We asked our calligrapher to redraw it making the character 'haá' more legible. We then created more fluidity to the characters giving greater visual appeal," Halton says.

A variety of metamorphoses of the existing icon then followed.

"When you start on a project like this, the development stage gets to a certain point when it may not reflect the existing logo. That is often productive as unexpected tangents often lead to the most creative solutions," the design director notes.

The final ABK logo is a mix of new and old. The bank's original icon was used as the jumping-off point to ensure a sense of continuity in the market.

The design team explored new directions to look at the bank's heritage and find a connection with regional history and modern branding. Extensive research uncovered a Persian mosaic on the façade of a mosque that contained geometric lines similar to the bank's original icon. The mosaic was redrawn and softened, with careful attention given to preserve the original mark's essence. The resulting icon provided the link to the bank's strong sense of cultural presence in the region.

The symbol's geometric shapes are interconnected, representing the concept of "coming together" for business and personal financial needs. "The new symbol is modern, yet it has a link to heritage and a connection to the old icon," says Halton. "It combines ABK's traditional corporate characteristics with a vibrant, innovative approach to modern banking."

Research into the competitor landscape led to further modifications. Origin chose to move away from the existing robust use of blue, which had previously been the primary color in collateral pieces and was the color most competitors used. The design team chose to differentiate the brand from its competitors by making yellow the new significant corporate color. In addition, the new brand uses substantial white space in collateral and signage to keep the system clean and uncluttered.

"By lightening the dark blue, and through the use of yellow, we softened the brand making its overall impression friendly and inviting. The ensuing logo refreshment led to further openness to change from ABK management," Halton says.

The new brand has been rolled out across all ABK's marketing collateral including credit cards, ATM screens, and websites, as well as branch signage and environmental graphics.

We tried a variety of directions, with the aim of coming up with a simple, clean icon that could be effectively reproduced on any modern medium.

"On a project of this nature, a lot of people within a company will become involved in the decision-making process, and this can hinder its progress. It is very important to get direct contact with the main decision maker," says Halton, "Because of this we successfully achieved the new brand rollout in a short space of time."

The two-way graphic wrap on the bank's head office building for the launch was the largest ever seen in Kuwait.

"Our launch campaign, 'the new face of banking,' reflects ABK's personality—modern, approachable, and open. Reception to the launch was extremely positive, and ABK consequently chose to air a TV commercial we produced during the Holy Month of Ramadan, which was based around the identity. The adverts show family and business people interacting around a huge scale model of the logo, which reinforces the idea of the bank being part of people's everyday lives," Halton says.

The aim of maintaining tradition and recognizability for existing clients while attracting new, younger clients was achieved, Halton says.

"While leaving a meeting in Kuwait, I overheard a comment that a new bank had recently opened. Knowing that this new bank is actually celebrating its fortieth year, I smiled to myself, job done," he adds.

Design team: Trevor Halton, Danesh Kondon, Shuma Rahman, Fahad Hawandaji, Maria Gaturian, Catalin Marin, John Harper Own, Binoy John

The new identity is very warm and inviting. Photography shows images from real life; the new color palette is also lively and fresh.

A large model of the interlocking logo was constructed for an ABK television commercial. It showed family and business people interacting around the new graphical identity.

Our launch campaign, 'the new face of banking,' reflects ABK's personality—modern, approachable, and open. Reception to the launch was extremely positive . . .

Design Firm	Hulsbosch Strategy and Design
Client	Woolworths
Project	Logo Design

Woolworths is by far the largest grocery chain in Australia with more than 780 stores, but it faces stiff competition. The company and its competitors have all grown significantly in the past several decades, but Woolworths stands out for being the most innovative and having remained consistent and strong with its marketing. "The Fresh Food People" tagline and accompanying jingle are as well known within the country as the kangaroo or koala.

Another big part of Woolworths' success is that its stores are run very much like family businesses: Many of the employees have been there for ten, twenty, thirty years, or more.

> They take their business personally. Part of their strength is that they are very passionate about what they do.

"They take their business personally. Part of their strength is that they are very passionate about what they do," explains Hans Hulsbosch, creative and managing director of Hulsbosch Strategy and Design (Sydney). Hulsbosch's team was invited by Woolworths' management to produce a logo that spoke directly of the key messages of the company—"fresh," "food," and "people"—but that was also clearly proprietary to Woolworths and no other grocery that might make similar claims. They would have six months in which to complete the project.

Hulsbosch began by considering the tagline: Did it still work for the company? His team researched the largest supermarkets in the world and studied their taglines and how they were used. After four weeks, he felt that the Woolworths tagline was quite possibly the best in use today and that it had the power to last another twenty years.

"The first two months of the project we had many discussions with management to truly understand their business and to us, their whole philosophy comes through in that one line," he says. "Therefore, its words became my guide in designing the new brand."

At the same time the Hulsbosch team was working on the project, the company was in the process of revamping all of their store interiors to make the shopping experience the best it can be (a process that will be completed in 2010). Wider aisles, natural textures, materials, and finishes gave the stores

Woolworths' previous logo, a tagline ("The Fresh Food People") run above the store name, was about twenty years old. Hans Hulsbosch of Hulsbosch Strategy and Design knew the client's tagline had great value and knew he would carry it into the new design. In this trial, the design is all about people. The heart-shaped fruit or vegetable looks friendly and open, while symbolizing fresh food.

This smiling concept conveyed the "people" part of the tagline.

Woolworths
the fresh food people

"This design was quite fun," says Hulsbosch. "This concept had six or seven different faces, all made out of fruit and vegetables."

Very modern in its design, this concept focused again on people. Bright colors suggest freshness and energy.

By placing two hearts together, Hulsbosch formed a *W* for Woolworths. The heart was also an evocative symbol that, in the context of the store, suggested that food is life.

Using a fresh green and orange, Hulsbosch here creates a human shape that is full of energy. In retrospect, he laughs about how similar it is to the new Walmart logo, which was released after the Woolworths' mark.

A *W*-shaped butterfly, emerging from a flower, creates a very positive, environmentally focused impression.

Woolworths
The fresh food people

Woolworths
The fresh food people

The shape of the final logo emerges in this trial. Hulsbosch liked the simplicity of the approach.

Woolworths
the fresh food people

(Above left) This very contemporary approach did not last long as it was felt to be too trendy and would age too quickly.

(Above right) The client liked this idea very much. The friendly, apron-clad grocer hearkened back to days when food was raised locally and was always fresh. But the concept was eventually discarded as too male.

(Left) This design is very close to the final, although it is flat. Here, the "people" element emerges in the shape of a person with upraised arms. The client requested green as the main color, although Hulsbosch felt that red is so important in retailing.

(Center) The logo is shown here in all green, but in one color, the leaf started to look like a candle flame instead.

(Left) Another variation with an additional leaf still wasn't quite right.

Woolworths
the fresh food people

The final design refers to fruit, freshness (through green), people (person with upraised arms) and the store name (W). Further viewing reveals another human shape: The leaf at top looks somewhat like a human head, tilted and looking down, toward arms curved in a caring posture.

a much more contemporary, inviting image. That twenty-first century feel also guided the designers in their work.

A final consideration comes from Hulsbosch's background in advertising and design. "I learned to work with identities so that they look right at the bottom of a print or TV ad, on a truck or on a pen. As I am designing, if I create something that won't look right at the end of a TV commercial, I throw it in the bin and start over," he says.

Hulsbosch's trials revolved around the key words and similar themes. For fresh, the color green was a must. It suggested nature, growth, and organic materials, as well as harmony and well-being.

The key word *food,* in relationship to the client's business, allowed the designers a great deal of play. They experimented with a variety of fruits and vegetables in his trials, noting that logos centered on food imagery would

be almost endless in their flexibility: The stores offered plenty of selections and, therefore, imagery.

Illustrating *people* in the new logo also presented plenty of opportunities. Hulsbosch tried actual and symbolic representations of people—an apron-clad grocer versus a heart, for example. Each held interest and potential, but Hulsbosch felt that he needed to tie all of the key words together.

His final solution not only represents all parts of "The Fresh Food People" in a single mark, but it also introduces a *W* for Woolworths, making the design ownable by the company. This final fact would allow the client to use the logo on its own, without the *Woolworths* name, on packaging, signage, uniforms, and other applications, when needed.

"The logo is first and foremost a *W,*" the designer says. "Its green color says 'fresh,' and what could be a fruit or a vegetable is part of the design.

Inside of the design is a person with outstretched arms. The leaf at the top represents positive thought."

In the final lockup, the color red is only used in the store name. "Red is the color of retail," says Hulsbosch. "It is the color of 'two for one,' and of lower prices. There is no doubt that Woolworths promotes itself through good value, but we didn't want to say 'cheap."

So red is only used in-store. "For outside signage, red will not be used. Instead, signage will be green and dark gray. The gray lifts the image of the brand in a wonderful way. It just zings off of the sign," the designer notes.

The rounded shapes in the design are very important to its success: They also say "nature" and "growth," as well as friendliness and caring.

The gradients in the rounded shapes and the color presented special challenges for signage. Not only are the problems associated with the transition from daylight to backlit night viewing, the Woolworths' management also wanted to reduce the amount of electricity it used and the heat

its signage threw into the atmosphere. So Hulsbosch and the Woolworths' team researched a range of options until they found a firm in the United States that could produce brilliant signage with a 70 percent reduction on the electricity cost and use.

With the logotype, the decision was to be simple and legible. This allows, over time, the logo to stand out, causing it to become the icon for Woolworths without the need for the typographic element. Ellen Lupton, a designer and writer of note on typography, puts it another way: "Although many books define the purpose of typography as enhancing the readability of the written word, one of design's most humane functions is, in actuality, to help readers avoid reading."

The new logo has all the attributes and personality of the Woolworths' brand not only for now but also as the brand moves forward into new and exciting phases of development. The simplicity and personable nature of the mark and the association with the essence of "fresh food people" will ensure the logo's longevity as the identifier of the brand Woolworths.

How the new Woolworths identity will be played out when fully implemented.

Qantas
Logo Redesign

Hulsbosch Strategy and Design, Sydney, Australia

Imagine being asked to redesign the best-known, best-loved logo in your own country. Imagine that the merest suggestion of such a redesign causes people—including design peers—to react in ways that range from nervous to clearly upset.

That's the dilemma faced by creative and managing director Hans Hulsbosch of Hulsbosch Strategy and Design in Sydney, Australia, when he began working with Qantas in 2006. The airline's kangaroo logo, originally designed in 1944 and updated in 1947, 1968, and 1984 (Hulsbosch also worked on that update), was not only revered in Australia, but is possibly the best-known Australian icon in the entire world.

"I knew it was going to be controversial," Hulsbosch says. "In 2006, the CEO of Qantas invited me for a 'chat' and told me that the company was investing in new Airbus A380 and Boeing 787 aircraft, to be delivered from 2008. He asked me to go to France and the U.S., where the new aircraft were being built and see if the old logo still worked on the new plane's body. During our conversation we both agreed that the old logo was tired and dated, but I had to have a very good reason for change and to design a new identity."

What Hulsbosch discovered after meeting with engineers in France, in the United States and Australia was that the aircraft tails in all new aviation design were becoming thinner and taller. The old kangaroo design would simply not fit into this new real estate without significant alteration of shape. Also, as the entire back horizontal stabilizer on the new planes move up and down, a large area is designated as a no-paint area due to scuffing.

"That meant that applying the old shape would cause the paint for the legs to be ruined right away, also giving the impression that the lower leg section was missing." Hulsbosch says.

These problems opened up the opportunity for a redesign. "We decided to change the kangaroo completely. In the old logo, designed back in 1944, the kangaroo is landing. Air travel is all about taking off and traveling somewhere," the designer says. Taking a lesson from the previous design, he also wanted to create an icon that allowed greater flexibility in all existing livery applications as well as accommodating future applications. He wanted to keep any paint added to the aircraft to a minimum as well, as paint adds weight, and weight adds to fuel costs. The gold trim feature was removed and the paint technology and application techniques were also changed to streamline costs.

The color red and the kangaroo were, of course, sacred and had to be kept. But Hulsbosch contemporized the animal a great deal. The animal is definitely moving: It has a more flowing, organic shape. The concept of streamlining the existing kangaroo was a constant thought during the early phases of the design.

The type that accompanies the mark was also redesigned. The custom-designed lettering leans dramatically forward. The shapes and forms mimic that of the kangaroo.

Qantas' new aircraft, complete with new livery, was delivered in September 2008. It was met with huge interest, discussion, and acclaim. Just recently, it was voted one of the ten best identities in the world at the Cannes Design Lion Awards in France.

"People have such a passion for this mark. Many designers think that it is one of the most powerful airline logos in the world," Hulsbosch says.

A variety of past Qantas logos (from left 1930s, 1940s, 1950s, and 1960s) reveal the heritage and visual inspiration of Hans Hulsbosch's new design.

The new Qantas logo not only fits the airline's newest aircraft better, it clearly maintains the continuity and national pride of previous marks.

collections and sketches

	A	B	C	D

1

LOGO SEARCH

Keywords | Initials |

Type: ○ Symbol ○ Typographic ○ Combo ● All

A.HUSET

2

AMUSE

ANDERSEN
CONCRETE

ALLÉCHANTE

3

АГЕНТСТВО
АЛИКА ЯКУБОВИЧА

4

ABACUS
GROUP

AVALANZ

ARGUMENT
YOUR COMFORTABLE LIFE

5

THE
BUCCANEER
CHARLESTON

bread&butter
country·store·restaurant

A B C D

1

2

3

4

5

Ⓓ = Design Firm   Ⓒ = Client

1A Ⓓ Anagraphic Ⓒ Bondavar   1B Ⓓ Karl Design Vienna Ⓒ ABC Zentrum Wien   1C Ⓓ Taxi Canada Ⓒ Brownstones Books   1D Ⓓ Banowetz + Company, Inc. Ⓒ Dr. Chuck Kobdish

2A Ⓓ Stygar Group, Inc. Ⓒ ButlerCook, LLP   2B Ⓓ Range   2C Ⓓ Sinclair & Co. Ⓒ Buric   2D Ⓓ Hoet & Hoet

3A Ⓓ Jeffhalmos Ⓒ Blaze Partners   3B Ⓓ Synergy Graphix Ⓒ Big Picture Blog   3C Ⓓ Fresh Oil Ⓒ Branek Construction   3D Ⓓ Designer Case Ⓒ Edipresse Polska S.A

4A Ⓓ DDB SF Ⓒ Clorox   4B Ⓓ L*U*K*E Ⓒ Cahill Financial Advisors   4C Ⓓ Hemmo.nl Ⓒ Corad Metal Recycling   4D Ⓓ MINE(tm) Ⓒ Post Carbon Institute

5A Ⓓ Skybend Ⓒ C Structures   5B Ⓓ bartodell.com Ⓒ critical   5C Ⓓ Sebastiany Branding & Design Ⓒ Pilkington & Saint Gobain   5D Ⓓ Gardner Design Ⓒ Catalyst

	A	B	C	D
1				
2				
3				
4				
5				

Ⓓ = Design Firm Ⓒ = Client

1A Ⓓ Gardner Design Ⓒ Collins Bus   1B Ⓓ Hubbell Design Works Ⓒ Costa Macaroni Manufacturing Co.   1C Ⓓ Hornall Anderson Ⓒ Coffee Bean & Tea Leaf   1D Ⓓ Whole Wheat Creative Ⓒ Children's Learning Institute

2A Ⓓ Christian Palino Design Ⓒ Cumberland Local Education Foundation   2B Ⓓ Porkka & Kuutsa Oy Ⓒ City of Helsinki Cultural Office   2C Ⓓ Gibson Ⓒ Carbon8 Systems   2D Ⓓ Gardner Design Ⓒ Catalyst

3A Ⓓ Landor Associates   3B Ⓓ Roy Smith Design Ⓒ Creative Audio   3C Ⓓ Pappas Group Ⓒ CSG Systems   3D Ⓓ Phony Lawn Ⓒ Chandler Design

4A Ⓓ Velocity Design Group Ⓒ Dixon Golf   4B Ⓓ Driving Force Ⓒ Driving Force   4C Ⓓ LogoDesignGuru.com Ⓒ Dynex Solution   4D Ⓓ Muamer Adilovic DESIGN Ⓒ SZR Dizajndziluk

5A Ⓓ BBDO NY Ⓒ DesignWorks at BBDO   5B Ⓓ Dennard, Lacey & Associates Ⓒ North Dallas   5C Ⓓ Steve Cantrell Ⓒ Diaz Multi Development   5D Ⓓ Brainchild Studios/NYC Ⓒ DC Comics

	A	B	C	D
1				
2				
3				
4				
5				

	A	B	C	D
1				
2				
3	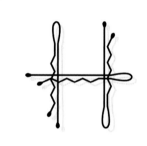			
4				
5				

D = Design Firm   C = Client

1A D Dennard, Lacey & Associates C Grand Homes   1B D 73ideas C Greystone Construction   1C D Mauck Groves Branding & Design C Griffith Homebuilders   1D D McGuire Design C Gilbert Brands

2A D Dennard, Lacey & Associates C Grand Homes   2B D Design Army C Goldman Law Group   2C D BRUEDESIGN C Garage Gym   2D D T H Gilmore C Self

3A D Oscar Morris C Hidden Salon   3B D Hazen Creative, Inc. C Hazen Creative, Inc.   3C D dache C Hashem Media   3D D Dotzero Design C House

4A D Diagram C Eligiuz   4B D Hand dizajn studio C Hand dizajn studio   4C D Gardner Design C Hullings Orthodontics   4D D Archrival C William Scully

5A D designheavy C Heartwood Guitar   5B D Headshot brand development C Headshot brand development   5C D moosylvania C Hyman Ltd.   5D D UlrichPinciotti Design Group

A   B   C   D

1

2

3

4

5

Ⓓ = Design Firm   Ⓒ = Client

1A Ⓓ Design Forum Ⓒ Holiday Inn   1B Ⓓ Hemmo.nl Ⓒ Heibro Gifts   1C Ⓓ Hirschmann Design Ⓒ Hirschmann Design   1D Ⓓ BFive Ⓒ Solo company

2A Ⓓ Hazen Creative, Inc. Ⓒ cre8, Inc. / Investors Observer   2B Ⓓ Heisel Design Ⓒ InsurePoint   2C Ⓓ Label Kings Ⓒ self-promotion   2D Ⓓ Launchpad Creative Ⓒ Granade Design

3A Ⓓ Rain Design Ⓒ Jackson Browne   3B Ⓓ Madomat Ⓒ Jo Jo Jam   3C Ⓓ dache Ⓒ K12 Reader   3D Ⓓ Team Y&R Ⓒ Khalid Bin Haider Group

4A Ⓓ UNIT-Y Ⓒ Kapstone Paper and Packaging Corporation   4B Ⓓ Oxide Design Co. Ⓒ Keen Guides   4C Ⓓ Brains on Fire Ⓒ Kaliburn   4D Ⓓ D&Dre Creative Ⓒ Karlson Construction

5A Ⓓ Karl Design Vienna Ⓒ Kolibri Kinderbuecherei   5B Ⓓ The Collaboration Ⓒ Kross Ink   5C Ⓓ King Design Office Ⓒ Ketti Handbags   5D Ⓓ dache Ⓒ K12 Reader

	A	B	C	D
1				
2				
3				
4				
5				

A   B   C   D

 método

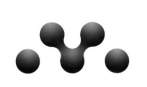

 MTK

1

 MONTANA CARDIOLOGY

2

 MILL VALLEY FILM FESTIVAL

3

 NATURHOME

 NORTHGATE

 numonyx™

4

 Nivasoft

netgRATUS

5

ⓓ = Design Firm ⓒ = Client

Ⓓ = Design Firm   Ⓒ = Client

1A Ⓓ Graphics & Designing Inc. Ⓒ Norio Yokokawa 1B Ⓓ The Right Hand Ⓒ NYC 1C Ⓓ face Ⓒ N8 Research 1D Ⓓ ODA Ⓒ Orqis

2A Ⓓ ohTwentyone Ⓒ Art of Opera Foundation 2B Ⓓ 73ideas Ⓒ Orele 2C Ⓓ Antoine Rodeghiero Ⓒ Online Concepts 2D Ⓓ Imadesign, Corp. Ⓒ Rosizo gallery

3A Ⓓ Caspari McCormick Ⓒ Polly's Palette Porter 3B Ⓓ Burocratik—Design Ⓒ Pixel Studio 3C Ⓓ elbow Ⓒ Plastic 3D Ⓓ reaves design Ⓒ NAS

4A Ⓓ Driving Force Ⓒ Bin Drai Enterprises 4B Ⓓ Actual Size Creative Ⓒ Powercast 4C Ⓓ Ivey McCoig Creative Partners Ⓒ Beat-Play 4D Ⓓ Roman Kotikov Ⓒ Plastic Republic

5A Ⓓ BrandBerry Ⓒ Qwell 5B Ⓓ Lippincott Ⓒ Quick Chek 5C Ⓓ Karl Design Vienna Ⓒ Braue / Q-Bioanalytic 5D Ⓓ Cassie Klingler Design

	A	B	C	D	
					1
					2
					3
					4
					5

	A	B	C	D
1				
2				
3				
4				
5				

	A	B	C	D	
1					1
2					2
3					3
4					4
5					5

Ⓓ = Design Firm Ⓒ = Client

1A Ⓓ Karl Design Vienna Ⓒ Truemmel Sanitaer Service 1B Ⓓ The Drawing Board Ⓒ TOP DOG GYMNASTICS 1C Ⓓ M3 Advertising Design Ⓒ Tisha Kim Casual Wear 1D Ⓓ POLLARDdesign Ⓒ Nike

2A Ⓓ Fiton Ⓒ Umhverfisstofnun 2B Ⓓ H2 Design of Texas Ⓒ unused 2C Ⓓ Herrainco Brand Strategy + Design Ⓒ unaVera Developments 2D Ⓓ D&Dre Creative Ⓒ Union Skate Park

3A Ⓓ R&R Partners Ⓒ Harrah's 3B Ⓓ Whaley Design, Ltd Ⓒ Visions Print Communications 3C Ⓓ Lippincott Ⓒ Vale 3D Ⓓ RDQLUS Creative Ⓒ VNDK8 Freestyle

4A Ⓓ Adstract Art Ⓒ Wallaston Wines 4B Ⓓ Fandam Studio Ⓒ Cellar d'Or 4C Ⓓ NOVOGRAMA Ⓒ Liquid Corp 4D Ⓓ King Design Office Ⓒ Wolfgang Puck Catering

5A Ⓓ Monster Design Company Ⓒ Workflow Office 5B Ⓓ Dragulescu Studio Ⓒ Nevada Cancer Institute, MGM/Mirage 5C Ⓓ The Office of Art+Logik Ⓒ Weidenbach Construction 5D Ⓓ Label Kings Ⓒ WILDLIFE

	A	B	C	D
1				
2				
3				
4				
5				(ZMEX BUSINESS CENTER)

🅳 = Design Firm 🅒 = Client

1A 🅳 Phony Lawn 🅒 Inkwell 1B 🅳 Pavone 🅒 Wright Photography 1C 🅳 Archrival 🅒 W Hair Studio 1D 🅳 Archrival 🅒 W Hair Studio

2A 🅳 Thermostat 🅒 Wettling Architects 2B 🅳 Vlad Ermolaev 🅒 Weave Music 2C 🅳 Habitat Design 🅒 West Meadows Construction 2D 🅒 S Design, Inc. 🅒 Big Industrial

3A 🅳 Tactix Creative 🅒 3B 🅳 Matchstic 🅒 X31 3C 🅳 Plumbline Studios 🅒 XeroCoat 3D 🅳 MUELLER design 🅒 MAXAMINE

4A 🅳 Mojo Solo 🅒 Proxama 4B 🅳 Kastelov 🅒 Yavaro 4C 🅳 Mattson Creative 🅒 YouthMinistry.com 4D 🅳 Dotzero Design 🅒 Your Half Pictures

5A 🅳 Nicole Ziegler 🅒 Zurich Wine Expo 5B 🅳 Toman Graphic Design 🅒 Z1 TV 5C 🅳 Snap Creative 🅒 Zupon Construction 5D 🅳 mIQelangelo 🅒 Zmex

	A	B	C	D	

          1

            2

            3

      SOCIETY27      4

      5

Reuters
Identity Design

Interbrand, New York, New York

The visual equity of the Reuters' dot was a must-keep when Interbrand created a new identity for the now-combined companies Reuters and Thomson. The static spiral has its own energy and movement, and the mark is easily animated.

When Thomson Corporation acquired Reuters in August 2007, the identity of the former could easily have overwhelmed the latter. The low-profile Canadian company Thomson was an enormous integrated information provider in the financial, scientific, health care, tax/accounting, and legal fields.

Reuters, on the other hand, was smaller although much better known as a leading financial news and media provider. When Interbrand was brought in to create a new identity for the new company, it was clear that while the Thomson identity did not have to be saved, the Reuters' mark definitely had valuable equity.

The Reuters' dot had particular brand heritage, three months of study by five different Interbrand offices revealed. "The research all centered around intelligent information and how it gives people the freedom to achieve. Information is a valuable commodity in today's market," says Interbrand creative director Jason Brown.

The research also revealed three pillars on which the new design was predicated: relevant depth, practical intuition, and immediate effectiveness. These were the aspects that the new company's clients would value most. In addition, the designers and client agreed that the company possessed the following personality attributes: optimistic, agile, human, and clear. These traits differed from other financial media organizations.

To convey the personality aspects, Brown's designers looked to patterns in nature—in particular, the Fibonacci sequence. The spiral is a common example of the sequence, but when patterned out in a series of larger and smaller dots, it also conveyed motion and a sense of energy—in other words, the way information is provided by the client.

The design team dubbed the new mark a "kinesis." "The dot is leveraged in the new mark, combined with the simple complexity of the patterns in nature," Brown explains. "The design is also literally forward-facing or moving."

The word mark is in a customized version of the typeface Neo Sans. The other face used in the identity is called Knowledge, a body text Interbrand created based on the face Locator. The use of all caps for the word mark feels clear and solid.

The primary color palette is based on plenty of white, with accents of an energetic orange and several shades of gray. A secondary palette of blue, red, and purple completes a suite of clear colors that Brown says were chosen for their optimistic nature.

The new mark lends itself easily to animation. Random dots flood together and organize into the kinesis, allowing the mark to physically demonstrate the flow of information provided by the client.

LOGO SEARCH

Keywords: **Typography**

Type: ○ Symbol ○ Typographic ○ Combo ● All

numb

!hey

wes

Set"

code

adcbe
Center for Dyslexic Studies

Muse

yard

bright ink

Дневник.ру

implant

ritual

segue

unusual

illiteracy

undertease

TouchFoundation

эhTⅼeonardo

Ⓓ = Design Firm   Ⓒ = Client

1C Ⓓ D&Dre Creative Ⓒ Numb Popsicle Stand   1D Ⓓ paralleldesigned Ⓒ ZEFER & !hey Software Inc.

2A Ⓓ www.admarc.com Ⓒ Wes Perry for Mayor   2B Ⓓ FutureBrand BC&H Ⓒ Set Investimentos   2C Ⓓ Manifest Communications Ⓒ CODE (formerly Canadian Organization for Development through Education)   2D Ⓓ julian peck Ⓒ Private

3A Ⓓ Kurt Snider Design Ⓒ Montage Resort   3B Ⓓ m|sane industries Ⓒ Yard Landshapers   3C Ⓓ moosylvania Ⓒ Bright Pink—Linsay Avner   3D Ⓓ Ulyanov Denis Ⓒ Dnevnik

4A Ⓓ Anagraphic Ⓒ Central Implant   4B Ⓓ MendeDesign Ⓒ Ritual Yoga   4C Ⓓ Kate Resnick Ⓒ Segue   4D Ⓓ Moker Ontwerp Ⓒ Business Unusual

5A Ⓓ Splash:Design Ⓒ Smile Africa   5B Ⓓ Eli Kirk Ⓒ Undertease   5C Ⓓ MSDS Ⓒ Touch Foundation   5D Ⓓ axiom design collaborative Ⓒ The Leonardo

	A	B	C	D
1	PHOTTOGRAPHY	WAGGING TONGUES	ATTICUS	
2	ZLAKI	FAIRYONAS	AMEROCK™	BLACK &BLUE
3	 FORO	AQUA APARTMENTS	SELECT WINES	 INKWELL
4	DUGENA		DEUX	FiVE DONS
5	ELKHORN	GREAT WEST	CASASIESTA RURAL LUXURY	

D = Design Firm   C = Client

Cleanwaste

explore

metro bike

bakelove BAKEWEAR

gangway

saxon

place.

starz

armeda

	A	B	C	D
1	 m‾nus	bl nk. sp ce	slice™	minim
2	Citelines	dialogue	McMillan Photography	stocktaking.ie food | beverage | retail
3	Verdigris	red yellow go!	BULL SHIT!	2Omaha
4	ATELIER	KONGFISK	MINGLE CONTRACTING INC	 TIVA
5	INVEST VIEW	E✳TRADE®	HIGHER PROMOTIONS	DIETHIN

	A	B	C	D	
	SAROS	FLOSS		WATER	1
	TIVIT IT Creativity	UMAMI うまみ	SAKE	LAVA™	2
	EDGE			EPIC	3
	L≡EVATION	AMEN		THERMOSTAT™	4
	SLICE	MESA GRILL	CAFE INSOMNIA	HOSPICE	5

Ⓓ = Design Firm   Ⓒ = Client

1A %OUTLET

1B BALANCE

1C  PARADOX

1D TUITIVE™

2A  SCOPE Database Management

2B EI8HT

2C SoHo

2D BIG NOISE PUBLIC RELATIONS

3A TORTURE

3B HUMIDOR FINE CIGARS

3C HALO

3D CASINOS

4A SPA CE clear experience

4B RIGH+LEFT

4C TRUEIT™

4D YIELD

5A  RED DELICIOUS

5B UNITY SHIRT

5C EARTH SHIFT EXPO™

5D PUBLIC ARCHITECTURE PUTS THE RESOURCES OF ARCHITECTURE IN THE SERVICE OF THE PUBLIC INTEREST. WE IDENTIFY AND SOLVE PRACTICAL PROBLEMS OF HUMAN INTERACTION IN THE BUILT ENVIRONMENT AND ACT AS A CATALYST FOR PUBLIC DISCOURSE THROUGH EDUCATION, ADVOCACY AND THE DESIGN OF PUBLIC SPACES AND AMENITIES. 1211 FOLSOM STREET, 4TH FLOOR, SAN FRANCISCO, CA 94103-3816 T 415.861.8200 F 415.431.9695 WWW.PUBLICARCHITECTURE.ORG

ChefBurger
Identity Design

Design Ranch, Kansas City, Missouri

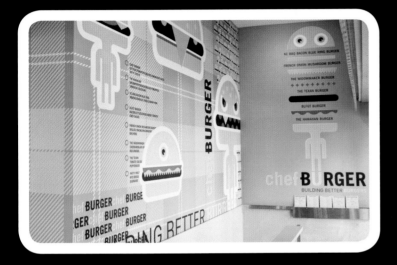

Design Ranch had the unique opportunity to create an all-encompassing brand identity for a new, upscale, fast-food restaurant called ChefBurger. From the store's architecture and interior to its food packaging and business stationery system, everything is tied together.

When a casual restaurant offers fare as interesting as falafel burgers, fried green beans, and spiked milkshakes, a diner knows right away that he or she is in for a completely different experience. Chef and entrepreneur Rob Dalzell dreamed up ChefBurger and its unique menu and hired Design Ranch to create an all-encompassing brand identity system that would perfectly match the food in terms of flavor and fun. Collaborating with McHenry Shaffer Architecture, the new identity is everywhere, from napkins, bags, and tabletops, to t-shirts, signage, and even the tissue paper that wraps each burger.

Located in Kansas City's Power and Light District, ChefBurger follows Dalzell's other restaurants in offering fabulous food, fresh ingredients, and great service, says principal Ingred Sidie. Customers can mix and match toppings and burgers endlessly, according to their specific tastes. "ChefBurger redefines the typical hamburger by offering unique and gourmet toppings in addition to simple signature items in a fun, casual environment," she says.

At the center of the new identity is the ChefBurger himself, a quirky icon influenced by urban culture and grown directly out of the restaurant's word mark. The designers explored other design directions as possibilities for the new identity, including an actual chef and a chef/bull, but these felt finite in concept. "We wanted an identity that was unexpected and original, one that uniquely conveyed customization," says senior designer Tad Carpenter.

The ChefBurger fits the bill. He has endless personalities. His face can be changed to suggest spicy, tangy, or just about any flavor. It can also suggest actual ingredients, such as bacon or veggies. He can have a body or not; he can be used with the word mark or alone; with a blue plaid background (chosen for its picnic/tablecloth implications) or on a solid color, white, or kraft paper bag background.

"We have created an iconic library for the brand. It provides visuals to draw upon to keep the brand fresh but controlled," says Design Ranch principal Michelle Sonderegger.

Originally, the client was leaning toward an all-type solution, to suggest that the restaurant is a bit more upscale. "But we felt he was missing an opportunity to create a recognizable and ownable brand—the icon needed to be there," she adds.

The word mark portion and the color of the identity further differentiate the business from other homogenized burger joints. "Many burger restaurants use red and yellow; we chose baby blue, which is much more modern. We also have a lot more metal, stainless, and light wood used in the finish and build out," adds Carpenter.

LOGO SEARCH

Keywords **Enclosures**

Type: ⚪ Symbol ⚪ Typographic ⚪ Combo ⦿ All

A B C D

    1

    2

    3

    4

    5

Ⓓ = Design Firm Ⓒ = Client

1A Ⓓ TOKY Branding+Design Ⓒ 100 Woodfire grille 1B Ⓓ TOKY Branding+Design Ⓒ 100 Woodfire grille 1C Ⓓ Special Modern Design Ⓒ Randi Hiller 1D Ⓓ Tower of Babel Ⓒ Dust Bunny House Cleaning

2A Ⓓ Collaboration Reverberation Ⓒ Evolve Online 2B Ⓓ northfound Ⓒ Catering St. Louis 2C Ⓓ Jon Flaming Design Ⓒ Gallery2 2D Ⓓ Filthy Clothing

3A Ⓓ King Design Office Ⓒ HiFi Project 3B Ⓓ Felixsockwell.com Ⓒ soViet Ⓒ Kamp Nokturnal 3D Ⓓ o.pudov Ⓒ Fund of Social Communications

4A Ⓓ Roy Smith Design Ⓒ Nicky Willcock Photography 4B Ⓓ Burocratik—Design Ⓒ 4C Ⓓ Tran Creative Ⓒ Interiors Northwest 4D Ⓓ Kommunikat Ⓒ Instytut Zdrowia i Urody

5A Ⓓ pearpod Ⓒ rsi 5B Ⓓ Jeffhalmos Ⓒ North Plains inc. 5C Ⓓ The Brand Agency Ⓒ landdevelopment.com.au 5D Ⓓ Hecht Design Ⓒ MIT Museum

93

	A	B	C	D
1				
2				
3				
4				
5				

1

2

3

4

5

Ⓓ = Design Firm   Ⓒ = Client

1A Ⓓ Tailor Designs Ⓒ LLC Ledovo 1B Ⓓ INDE Ⓒ Personal 1C Ⓓ Dotzero Design Ⓒ Afrique Bistro 1D Ⓓ Yaroslav Zheleznyakov Ⓒ Lemonades from Arbuzov

2A Ⓓ Vasco Morelli Design Ⓒ Thread Communications 2B Ⓓ RIZN Communication Design Ⓒ Silver Noise 2C Ⓓ Gardner Design Ⓒ coleman 2D Ⓓ 903 Creative, LLC Ⓒ 903 Creative

3A Ⓓ 13THFLOOR Ⓒ A-HA Entertainment 3B Ⓓ BBMG Ⓒ Case Foundation 3C Ⓓ Gesture Studio Ⓒ Isaias Gil 3D Ⓓ Skin Designstudio Ⓒ Photographer Bjorn-Eivind Aartun

4A Ⓓ BBDO NY Ⓒ King Low Heywood Thomas School 4B Ⓓ CAPSULE Ⓒ Minnesota Lightning Professional Soccer Club 4C Ⓓ Campbell Fisher Design Ⓒ Grand Prix Arizona 4D Ⓓ Mindpower Inc. Ⓒ Historic Oakland Foundation

5A Ⓓ GDNSS Ⓒ cheapairlines.com 5B Ⓓ Fifth Letter Ⓒ Caffe Prada 5C Ⓓ Tandemodus Ⓒ Cycle Touring Outfitters 5D Ⓓ Schwartzrock Graphic Arts Ⓒ Cross Culture Entertainment

LOGO SEARCH

Keywords: **Display Type**

Type: ⊙ Symbol ⊙ Typographic ⊙ Combo ⦿ All

A	B	C	D	
				1
				2
				3
				4
				5

Ⓓ = Design Firm   Ⓒ = Client

	A	B	C	D
1		**baga** BATHROOM AND DESIGN ATELIER	PsD	Carrot
2		UCan	DUNN	SUPERFLY
3		my Kangoo	FuDYDuD	BEACH BEING
4	 PASSION FOR FOOD	THE THIEVES	ShortHanded	MOCA UNDERGROUND
5	cristal	EPICENTER	FUEGO	WILD WEST ICE CREAM COMPANY

Ⓓ = Design Firm   Ⓒ = Client

1A Ⓓ Pearson Education Ltd Ⓒ Pearson Education 1B Ⓓ Josef Stapel Ⓒ BADA 1C Ⓓ Vlad Ermolaev Ⓒ Russian Railways 1D Ⓓ Hula+Hula Ⓒ Carrot Skateboards

2A Ⓓ Valhalla | Design & Conquer Ⓒ Adio Shoes 2B Ⓓ Cubic Ⓒ Cody Haltom Ⓒ Casey Dunn 2D Ⓓ Karl Design Vienna Ⓒ Spirit / Superfly Radio GmbH

3A Ⓓ Glitschka Studios Ⓒ Street Value 3B Ⓓ Studio Limbus Ⓒ United Experts 3C Ⓓ Jeff Andrews Design Ⓒ Fuddydud 3D Ⓓ nGen Works Ⓒ Beach Being

4A Ⓓ reaves design Ⓒ kraft 4B Ⓓ Schwartzrock Graphic Arts Ⓒ Community Comics 4C Ⓓ Nissen Design Ⓒ Shorthanded (band) 4D Ⓓ Michael O'Connell Ⓒ Museum of Contemporary Art Jacksonville

5A Ⓓ Wox Ⓒ Alan Almeida 5B Ⓓ Stuph Clothing Ⓒ Amarillo Hillside Christian Church 5C Ⓓ The Laster Group Ⓒ El Paso Museum of Art 5D Ⓓ Arsenal Design, Inc. Ⓒ Wild West Ice Cream Company

	A	B	C	D
1			pba	 unfold
2				
3	 FORGE CONSTRUCTIONS			NEU SCHOOL OF ARCHITECTURE
4	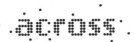			
5				

LOGO SEARCH

Keywords **Calligraphy**

Type: ○ Symbol ○ Typographic ○ Combo ● All

Ⓓ = Design Firm Ⓒ = Client

1C Ⓓ Tower of Babel Ⓒ Tower of Babel   1D Ⓓ Hula+Hula Ⓒ Stagecoach / Goldenvoice

2A Ⓓ CF Napa Brand Design Ⓒ Sea Smoke Cellars   2B Ⓓ David Beck Design Ⓒ Tina Marie Rabb, writer   2C Ⓓ Rocketlab Creative Ⓒ Estella Albion   2D Ⓓ Schwartzrock Graphic Arts Ⓒ Infinity Direct

3A Ⓓ Westwerk DSGN Ⓒ Shauna Style   3B Ⓓ Opolis Design, LLC Ⓒ Thread   3C Ⓓ Moker Ontwerp Ⓒ Soul Kitchen   3D Ⓓ Digital Slant Ⓒ Shundahai

4A Ⓓ NOT A CANNED HAM Ⓒ Avon   4B Ⓓ Mitre Agency Ⓒ Hanberry's   4C Ⓓ Octavo Designs Ⓒ The Perfect Truffle   4D Ⓓ KTD Ⓒ Pace Foods

5A Ⓓ Squires and Company Ⓒ XTO Energy   5B Ⓓ Sebastiany Branding & Design Ⓒ Cinecittá caffe   5C Ⓓ 13thirtyone Design Ⓒ Ambiance   5D Ⓓ Yaroslav Zheleznyakov Ⓒ Ice work

100

1

2

3

4

5

D = Design Firm   **C** = Client

1A **D** Gardner Design **C** Neil Young, Johnathan Goodwin   1B **D** supersoon good design **C** LucyLuke, Australia   1C **D** HOOK **C** Zanzibar   1D **D** Dessein **C** Department of Culture and Arts

2A **D** Zieldesign **C** Deborah Pearcy   2B **D** Dill and Company **C** Gilt Parcels   2C **D** Banowetz + Company, Inc. **C** Criterion Development Partners   2D **D** Sunrise Advertising **C** Cincinnati Playhouse in the Park

3A **D** Entermotion Design Studio **C** Sugar   3B **D** Brian Krezel **C** Ripcurl   3C **D** BrandBerry **C** Ctulhu   3D **D** Ginter & Miletina **C** self

4A **D** Denis Olenik Design Studio **C** Gotovim.ru   4B **D** Park Avenue Design **C** Zinelli   4C **D** Skybend **C** Von Roxy   4D **D** HOOK **C** Blend

5A **D** Relevant Studio **C** Tango Eyewear   5B **D** Prana Design + Art Studios **C** Escobar Lounge + Bar   5C **D** Advertising Intelligence **C** Restaurant   5D **D** Christian Hanson **C** Fusion Mate De Coca

Ogulin Fairy Tale Festival
Logo Design

Studio Cuculić, Zagreb, Croatia

The work of Studio Cuculić, a design firm located in Zagreb, Croatia, is split between commercial and cultural clients. The three-designer shop enjoys working in both directions but is especially known for its cultural work, including clients such as Gavella Drama Theatre, Dance and Non-verbal Theatre Festival San Vincenti, and Museum Lapidarium.

In 2007, the design firm created a charming set of logos for the Ogulin Fairy Tale Festival, which earned them special attention. The festival, held in Ogulin, Croatia, is the birthplace of one of Croatia's top writers, the late I. B. Mazuranic. Mazuranic is recognized as one of Croatia's best writers for children: She was twice nominated for the Nobel Prize and was also the first woman to be accepted into the Croatian Academy of Sciences and Art.

Her fairy tales, written in the early 1900s, are beloved by adults and children alike, so much so that the festival draws several thousands of people each year. National and international artists, performers, and lecturers also attend. The event has become a very popular event, requiring its own marketing and identity.

The author's tales were inspired by legends local to Ogulin and by the natural environment of the area. Each story paints its own elaborate and much-loved picture: Each story is special. So a single logo could hardly encompass the richness and content of all of the tales. Instead, Studio Cuculić designers created a multiple logo system.

"They all have their stories, [with each character] being a leading role, and in that way, they are equally important," says Zeljka Pencinger of Studio Cuculić.

Each of the six characters is actually a multiple personality. Other, secondary characters from the stories are embedded directly into the fantastical body shapes.

"This solution is very attractive and interesting for the client, as well as for the visitors of the festival, especially kids," says Pencinger. "On first sight, the logos seem to be simple, but they are indeed complex-characters hidden inside of other characters just to tease you to see what else her stories and the festival have to offer. What else is hidden and needs to be unveiled?"

In addition to being reproduced in printed materials in a rich palette that includes gradated shades of orange, purple, green, blue, and red, the character shapes were also cut from clear Plexiglas and placed throughout Ogulin and its surroundings in places where, according to legend, magical events and stories took place. This is a permanently installed set of designs that create a theme route, which can be visited individually or with a guide through the whole year. The logos are also used on souvenirs as well as small print material that promote the festival.

LOGO SEARCH

Keywords **Crests**

Type: ◯ Symbol ◯ Typographic ◯ Combo ◉ All

A   B   C   D

1

2

3

(SOL logo)

4

5

Ⓓ = Design Firm   Ⓒ = Client

1C Ⓓ bartodell.com Ⓒ McKay's Bakery   1D Ⓓ Gardner Design Ⓒ Lavish Boutique

2A Ⓓ Velocity Design Group Ⓒ NaturalBreed Con,   2B Ⓓ Stygar Group, Inc. Ⓒ The Enlighten Baker   2C Ⓓ Mitre Agency Ⓒ Finnigan's Wake   2D Ⓓ McDill Design Ⓒ Irish Festivals Inc.

3A Ⓓ Tim Frame Design Ⓒ touristees.com   3B Ⓓ DUSTIN PARKER ARTS Ⓒ STACY RINK   3C Ⓓ Marlin Ⓒ The Marlin Company   3D Ⓓ Hill Design Studios Ⓒ Oregon Valley Boys

4A Ⓓ Velocity Design Group Ⓒ Schnepf Farms   4B Ⓓ Dennard, Lacey & Associates Ⓒ Crawford Farms   4C Ⓓ Trapdoor Studio Ⓒ Sons of Liberty   4D Ⓓ Tim Frame Design Ⓒ Dennis Miller Show

5A Ⓓ David Beck Design Ⓒ Phil Romano   5B Ⓓ Home Grown Logos Ⓒ Azz & Bzz Apparel   5C Ⓓ bailey brand consulting Ⓒ Compass Group International   5D Ⓓ Jon Kay Design Ⓒ Starmen.Net

	A	B	C	D
1				
2				
3				
4				
5				

Ⓓ = Design Firm   Ⓒ = Client

<table>
<tr><td></td><td>A</td><td>B</td><td>C</td><td>D</td></tr>
</table>

A   **B**   **C**   **D**

      **1**

     **2**

      **3**

      **4**

      **5**

Ⓓ = Design Firm   Ⓒ = Client

1A Ⓓ Mitre Agency Ⓒ Krispy Kreme   1B Ⓓ The Office of Art+Logik Ⓒ Weidenbach Concrete Works   1C Ⓓ Erwin-Penland, Inc. Ⓒ Nuvox & Greenville Drive Baseball   1D Ⓓ RWest Ⓒ BridgePort Brewery

2A Ⓓ Struck Ⓒ Dynamic Confections   2B Ⓓ CF Napa Brand Design Ⓒ Judy's Candies   2C Ⓓ Inertia Graphics Ⓒ Boone Electric   2D Ⓓ RARE Design Ⓒ Leatha's

3A Ⓓ Kolar Advertising and Marketing Ⓒ Southside Market & BBQ   3B Ⓓ Bailey Lauerman 2 Ⓒ   3C Ⓓ Oliver Russell Ⓒ Idaho Ski Areas Association   3D Ⓓ Envision Creative Group Ⓒ Let Them Eat Cupcakes

4A Ⓓ Sussner Design Company Ⓒ pardon my french bakery   4B Ⓓ McDill Design Ⓒ Miller Brewing Company   4C Ⓓ Gardner Design Ⓒ Piccadilly   4D Ⓓ Tower of Babel Ⓒ Tower of Babel

5A Ⓓ Velocity Design Group Ⓒ Schnepf Farms   5B Ⓓ Velocity Design Group Ⓒ Whole Grain Natural Bread Co.   5C Ⓓ Entermotion Design Studio Ⓒ Bradshaw Kirchofer   5D Ⓓ Strategic America Ⓒ Iowa Farm Bureau Federation

	A	B	C	D
1				
2				
3				
4				
5				

Ⓓ = Design Firm Ⓒ = Client

1A Ⓓ Oomingmak Design Company Ⓒ Donruss Trading Card Company   1B Ⓓ Mindspike Design Ⓒ Pinahs Snack Co.   1C Ⓓ Cricket Design Works Ⓒ Sardine   1D Ⓓ Wox Ⓒ FABIO PEDRO

2A Ⓓ Iperdesign, Inc. Ⓒ willig's taverna   2B Ⓓ TOKY Branding+Design Ⓒ Food Outreach of St. Louis   2C Ⓓ three Ⓒ Southeastern Horticultural Society   2D Ⓓ Chris Rooney Illustration/Design Ⓒ San Francisco Film Society

3A Ⓓ Tower of Babel Ⓒ The Flower Company   3B Ⓓ Phony Lawn Ⓒ Monteverdi   3C Ⓓ Phony Lawn Ⓒ Monteverdi   3D Ⓓ Dragulescu Studio Ⓒ Palms Casino and Hotel

4A Ⓓ UNIT-Y Ⓒ Gerard Design   4B Ⓓ Design Farm Ⓒ Hot Wheels   4C Ⓓ Sayles Graphic Design, Inc. Ⓒ Iron Hearse   4D Ⓓ Swanson Russell Ⓒ Shindaiwa

5A Ⓓ The Eppstein Group Ⓒ Fort Worth Republican Women   5B Ⓓ Dennard, Lacey & Associates Ⓒ Bennigan's Tavern & Grill   5C Ⓓ RedBrand Ⓒ PLSE   5D Ⓓ 2TREES DESIGN Ⓒ 2TREES DESIGN

Østerbro
Logo Design

Søren Severin, Denmark, Copenhagen

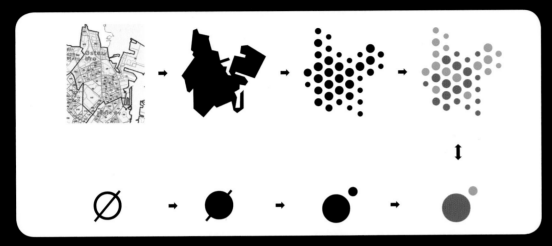

(Left) This progression shows how designer Søren Severin took advantage of the unusual shape of the Østerbro district as well as the Ø in its name to create a highly unique identity for the borough in Denmark. (Right) The final Østerbro lockup.

Søren Severin was on the wrong side of the world when a prestigious student logo design competition was announced at The Danish Designschool (DKDS) in Copenhagen. He was enjoying a semester as an exchange student at the Rhode Island School of Design and learned about the competition via an e-mail sent to all DKDS students. Although he missed the actual briefing, he decided to enter anyway—a fortunate decision as Severin's design solution was eventually chosen as the winner.

The competition asked entrants to design a logo for the borough of Østerbro. In 2006, the city council of Copenhagen decided to establish individual city district counsels for each of its boroughs. By the end of 2008, there will be twelve local districts, of which Østerbro is one. The new local council of Østerbro wanted to stand out and strengthen its visual identity, so it opened up the logo design opportunity to local design school students and made it worth their while: DKK 50.000 ($10,000 U.S.) total prize money would be given to the winners.

The written brief asked that the logo detail distinctive characteristics of Østerbro, but what exactly this meant was left up to the designer. As the district is considered to be one of the more conservative areas in Copenhagen, he briefly considered a coat of arms as a traditional identity symbol.

"But I abandoned that idea because I decided that I didn't want to speculate into what I thought they wanted and so underestimate the client's amenability," Severin recalls. "I would rather do something original that I thought was interesting and hope that the client would be open to something more unorthodox."

So another direction developed. Severin was working on his own portfolio website at the time and had been experimenting with the special Danish letter ø, which is used in his name.

"Since this letter is distinctive, it contains a lot of identity that can be used in a logo. Also, the major local districts of Copenhagen-City, North bridge, West bridge, and East bridge—are locally known as C, N, V, and Ø. So the character Ø was already a well-known characteristic for the district," Severin explains.

The use of the dot also connected the design to the graphical representation of the logo. Severin transformed the actual geographical shape of the district into a raster pattern made of large dots. Everything ties back to the round "o" letterforms in the district's name.

LOGO SEARCH

Keywords | **Sports**

Type: ○ Symbol ○ Typographic ○ Combo ● All

Ⓓ = Design Firm   Ⓒ = Client

1C Ⓓ Studio Simon Ⓒ Wladyka Baseball   1D Ⓓ Brandon Hall Ⓒ New York Penn League

2A Ⓓ Bryan Cooper Design Ⓒ Red Barons Baskball   2B Ⓓ VanPaul Design Ⓒ Steve Ellis   2C Ⓓ Studio Simon Ⓒ Minor League Baseball   2D Ⓓ Studio Simon Ⓒ Billings Mustangs

3A Ⓓ Hiebing Ⓒ Hiebing   3B Ⓓ Jon Kay Design Ⓒ Starmen.Net   3C Ⓓ Traction Ⓒ NBA D-League   3D Ⓓ Gary Sample Design Ⓒ Madness Sports

4A Ⓓ Torch Creative Ⓒ NBA Entertainment   4B Ⓓ RARE Design Ⓒ Nike   4C Ⓓ Label Kings Ⓒ FACEHOOP   4D Ⓓ XYNTFK Ⓒ VBA

5A Ⓓ RARE Design Ⓒ Lone Star Sports and Entertainment   5B Ⓓ Hotwire, Inc Ⓒ ABC Sports   5C Ⓓ Hotwire, Inc Ⓒ ABC Sports   5D Ⓓ Steve Cantrell Ⓒ Professional Football Chiropractic

A	B	C	D

     1

    2

      3

      4

      5

ⓓ = Design Firm   ⓒ = Client

1A ⓓ Fiton ⓒ N1   1B ⓓ Design Farm ⓒ Precision Tees   1C ⓓ vladimir sijerkovic ⓒ Golf Republic   1D ⓓ Schwartzrock Graphic Arts ⓒ Infinity Direct

2A ⓓ Rhombus, Inc. ⓒ John Zimmerman   2B ⓓ LEKKERWERKEN ⓒ Deutscher Golf Verband   2C ⓓ Liquid Inc ⓒ Indian Hills Golf Club   2D ⓓ Michael Patrick Partners ⓒ Michael Patrick Partners

3A ⓓ Severance Digital Studio   3B ⓓ 903 Creative, LLC ⓒ S.H. United   3C ⓓ McGuire Design ⓒ The Flying Medranos   3D ⓓ The Bradford Lawton Design Group ⓒ Shavanno Park Tennis Club

4A ⓓ pearpod ⓒ ski for good   4B ⓓ Burton (Snowboards) Corp. ⓒ Burton Snowboards   4C ⓓ ezzo Design ⓒ Surf Local   4D ⓓ Roy Smith Design ⓒ surfindex

5A ⓓ Driving Force ⓒ Dubai Surfski and Kayak Club   5B ⓓ mod&co ⓒ City Canoe   5C ⓓ LEKKERWERKEN ⓒ Oliver Foerster   5D ⓓ POLLARDdesign ⓒ Nike

LOGO SEARCH

Keywords **Heads**

Type: ○ Symbol   ○ Typographic   ○ Combo   ● All

Ⓓ = Design Firm   Ⓒ = Client

1C Ⓓ Chris Rooney Illustration/Design Ⓒ Heavenly Ski Resort   1D Ⓓ Tactix Creative Ⓒ Yum Brands

2A Ⓓ Chris Rooney Illustration/Design Ⓒ Chris Rooney   2B Ⓓ RARE Design Ⓒ Elvis Presley Enterprises   2C Ⓓ elbow Ⓒ Digital Guilt   2D Ⓓ Image Public, Inc. Ⓒ URBAN HEAD

3A Ⓓ Phixative Ⓒ Burp Armor   3B Ⓓ Bryan Cooper Design Ⓒ Tulsa Children's Museum   3C Ⓓ POLLARDdesign Ⓒ Lily Creative Group   3D Ⓓ Kolar Advertising and Marketing Ⓒ Amarillo National Bank

4A Ⓓ VanPaul Design Ⓒ StackOverflow.com   4B Ⓓ Karl Design Vienna Ⓒ Burmahilfe Austria   4C Ⓓ Glitschka Studios Ⓒ HGTV   4D Ⓓ VanPaul Design Ⓒ HousePriceSpy.com

5A Ⓓ Squires and Company Ⓒ Domtar   5B Ⓓ Mojo Solo Ⓒ West Publishing   5C Ⓓ dache Ⓒ Think Once   5D Ⓓ Gardner Design Ⓒ authentus

A B C D

1

2

3

4

5

1

2

3

4

5

Ⓓ = Design Firm   Ⓒ = Client

1A Ⓓ Oscar Morris Ⓒ Parmer Lane Tavern   1B Ⓓ Worth | Design Ⓒ Arizona Science Center   1C Ⓓ moosylvania Ⓒ Johnny's Lunch   1D Ⓓ Schwartzrock Graphic Arts Ⓒ Rightway Auto Glass

2A Ⓓ Nectar Graphics Ⓒ Ella Bees Jewelry   2B Ⓓ A3 Design Ⓒ TargetCare   2C Ⓓ Bryan Cooper Design Ⓒ Conquest   2D Ⓓ Hero Design Studio Ⓒ Tandem Brand

3A Ⓓ Bailey Lauerman 2   3B Ⓓ Essex Two Ⓒ Hyde Park Jazz Festival & The University of Chicago   3C Ⓓ DUSTIN PARKER ARTS Ⓒ SCORCHES SALSA   3D Ⓓ ulitenko Ⓒ Larussia

4A Ⓓ LEKKERWERKEN Ⓒ Lekkerwerken   4B Ⓓ Glitschka Studios Ⓒ Upper Deck Company   4C Ⓓ The Robin Shepherd Group Ⓒ Half Moon Bay Trading Co.   4D Ⓓ jenn gula design Ⓒ California Greens

5A Ⓓ Glitschka Studios Ⓒ Barbara Vick Design   5B Ⓓ Glitschka Studios Ⓒ Barbara Vick Design   5C Ⓓ Glitschka Studios Ⓒ Upper Deck Company   5D Ⓓ Glitschka Studios Ⓒ Rob Schwager

A	B	C	D	
	 			1
				2
				3
				4
				5

Ⓓ = Design Firm   Ⓒ = Client

1A Ⓓ Lizette Gecel Ⓒ Brand Facilitators 1B Ⓓ R&R Partners Ⓒ Zappos 1C Ⓓ Kloom Ⓒ Essociate 1D Ⓓ Mauck Groves Branding & Design Ⓒ Poindexter [Print Intelligence]

2A Ⓓ Worth | Design Ⓒ Water Wise 2B Ⓓ Karl Design Vienna Ⓒ ABC Zentrum Wien 2C Ⓓ Jerron Ames Ⓒ Arteis 2D Ⓓ mugur mihai Ⓒ NetOptical

3A Ⓓ Beveridge Seay, Inc. Ⓒ Duet Incorporated 3B Ⓓ Shawn Huff Ⓒ McMillian Family 3C Ⓓ Aline Forastieri Ⓒ Unused 3D Ⓓ Squires and Company Ⓒ Texas Bike Association

4A Ⓓ Darkstone&Cardinal Ⓒ Mr. Caries 4B Ⓓ Murillo Design, Inc. Ⓒ Murillo Design, Inc. 4C Ⓓ Red Olive Design Ⓒ Fruition 4D Ⓓ Gyula Németh Ⓒ glimpses.tv

5A Ⓓ APSITS Ⓒ DIESEL 5B Ⓓ Hirschmann Design Ⓒ Rob Nagler & Jonathan Sandberg 5C Ⓓ Integrated Communications (ICLA) Ⓒ Squint 5D Ⓓ Helius Creative Advertising Ⓒ RekognEYES Marketing

Fitness Experience/Gold's Gym
Logo Design

Von Glitschka, Salem, Oregon

When a team of long-time Gold Gym's franchise owners in Salem, Oregon, decided that their experience and talents could support the opening of their own gym, Fitness Experience, they knew exactly what they wanted in a new logo—or, at least, they thought they did.

Of course, their business was all about health and vitality. But designer Von Glitschka could see another level of benefit to their work.

"What is the final goal of the people going to the gym?" he asked himself. "I didn't think we should focus on what they do at the gym. It's not about a little muscle guy lifting weights, like in the Gold's Gym logo: I definitely wanted to avoid that and told the client it was not right for them. The question should be: What do people really want from working out?"

Glitschka had in mind a logo that was more of a sports mark than a gym logo. He also wanted a very simple, flat mark that could work anywhere-on a t-shirt, in embroidery, on a screen, anywhere.

"At the gym, the employees can come right alongside the customer and train them. It's a very simple process, not complex at all. The act of working out is hard, though, and that's what I wanted to pick up on—being lean and mean," he says.

The designer created five different comps for the client. One design contained the actual shape of a human in action—sort of in step aerobics mode. Another (created by friend and designer Jeff Nine, who he brought into the project for consultation) used a red circle to contain an abstracted *F* that mimicked a heart rate display on a screen.

A design that showed a human form with outstretched arms had good proportions, Glitschka felt, but he didn't believe it said much

about fitness. "It was a bit too futuristic," he says, "probably better for a Star Trek uniform."

The final two designs were the ones the clients liked best. The one they were leaning to combined the letterforms *F* and *E*. It canted forward, suggesting action in its solid, muscular form. It worked as a word mark as well as a sports mark, as Glitschka wanted, but he felt his final solution was still the best one.

"I wanted movement and activeness—that's where the wing comes in. But it also builds in the hidden *E* and *F*. The shape of the shield I modeled after the human torso," he explains. For color, he selected green to suggest health and fitness. "Other fitness groups were using plenty of red, so I pushed in the other direction." A benefit to the minty green he selected is that it shifts very little in tone whether it is on a black or a white background.

Von Glitschka's first trial design for Fitness Experience had a step aerobics feel.

This monogram design suggested action with its forward lean.

The designers liked the proportions of this design but felt it was a bit too futuristic.

This experiment is a monogram, but it also displays a wing shape. The designer wanted the client to have a solid icon that could be used on t-shirts, signage and other marketing materials.

LOGO SEARCH

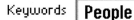

Keywords **People**

Type: ○ Symbol ○ Typographic ○ Combo ● All

AQUASIS

Sculptors

BELABUMBUM
Handmade in Brazil
FOUNDED IN 2001
LINGERIE & MATERNITY

Water for **Africa**

TORONTO LYRIC SYMPHONY

SLICE
PIZZA

Flathau's Fine Foods

LE BON BONBON
NAPOLEON

Eco-Services

LECTURE   SERIES
FAITH
& LIFE

ⓓ = Design Firm   ⓒ = Client

1C ⓓ Yaroslav Zheleznyakov ⓒ a public social organization   1D ⓓ Dotzero Design ⓒ Sad Sacks and Cats

2A ⓓ Bailey Lauerman 2   2B ⓓ Art Libera, ZAMBEZY ID ⓒ Sculptors   2C ⓓ Gardner Design ⓒ Belabumbum   2D ⓓ Diagram

3A ⓓ Dennard, Lacey & Associates ⓒ Toronto Lyric Symphony   3B ⓓ Hornall Anderson ⓒ Holland America Line   3C ⓓ RARE Design ⓒ Flathau's Fine Foods   3D ⓓ Graphic Nincompoop ⓒ Matarast

4A ⓓ Opolis Design, LLC ⓒ Baby Jogger   4B ⓓ 01D ⓒ Sushcof   4C ⓓ POLLARDdesign ⓒ Rain Direct Marketing   4D ⓓ Ray Dugas Design

5A ⓓ pictogram studio ⓒ Pictogram Studio   5B ⓓ Today ⓒ Napoleon   5C ⓓ Tactix Creative ⓒ US Postal Service   5D ⓓ Schwartzrock Graphic Arts ⓒ Mt. Olivet Lutheran Church

<table>
<tr>
<th></th><th>A</th><th>B</th><th>C</th><th>D</th>
</tr>
<tr>
<td>1</td>
<td></td>
<td></td>
<td></td>
<td></td>
</tr>
<tr>
<td>2</td>
<td></td>
<td></td>
<td></td>
<td></td>
</tr>
<tr>
<td>3</td>
<td></td>
<td></td>
<td></td>
<td></td>
</tr>
<tr>
<td>4</td>
<td></td>
<td></td>
<td></td>
<td></td>
</tr>
<tr>
<td>5</td>
<td></td>
<td></td>
<td></td>
<td></td>
</tr>
</table>

Ⓓ = Design Firm   Ⓒ = Client

1A Ⓓ Schwartzrock Graphic Arts Ⓒ Enhanced Landscaping   1B Ⓓ Schwartzrock Graphic Arts Ⓒ American Bible Society   1C Ⓓ Schwartzrock Graphic Arts Ⓒ Catalyst Studios   1D Ⓓ Schwartzrock Graphic Arts Ⓒ American Bible Society

2A Ⓓ Haley Johnson Design Co. Ⓒ Fizzy Lizzy   2B Ⓓ Greteman Group Ⓒ City of Wichita   2C Ⓓ Lightship Visual Ⓒ comiczone   2D Ⓓ NeoGrafica Ⓒ Ragga by Roots

3A Ⓓ Franke+Fiorella Ⓒ Hestia Heating Products   3B Ⓓ 13thirtyone Design Ⓒ The Modern Woman's Divorce Guide   3C Ⓓ joni dunbar design Ⓒ Missyanna's   3D Ⓓ Nynas

4A Ⓓ Nynas Ⓒ Rockwall Preschool Association   4B Ⓓ Banowetz + Company, Inc. Ⓒ NorthPark Center   4C Ⓓ Riley Designs Ⓒ Heiny Hiders   4D Ⓓ studio sudar d.o.o. Ⓒ gluteus maximus d.o.o.

5A Ⓓ Patten ID Ⓒ Dana Patten   5B Ⓓ Artista Muvek Ⓒ Cafe Kockas Baro   5C Ⓓ Schwartzrock Graphic Arts Ⓒ Heartland Wood Products   5D Ⓓ Sabingrafik, Inc. Ⓒ Seafarer Baking Company

	A	B	C	D
1				
2				
3				
4				
5				

1

2

FANCY
PANTS
PRESS

3

4

5

1

2

3

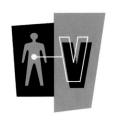

4

5

	A	B	C	D
1				
2				
3	 **FREESTYLE**			
4				
5				

Ⓓ = Design Firm   Ⓒ = Client

1A Ⓓ legofish Ⓒ Quad Info Tech   1B Ⓓ Bailey Lauerman 2   1C Ⓓ Schwartzrock Graphic Arts Ⓒ Design Center   1D Ⓓ Willoughby Design Group Ⓒ The United Nations

2A Ⓓ Honey Design Ⓒ Private Health Solutions   2B Ⓓ DAGSVERK—Design and Advertising Ⓒ Lagafell Sports Centre   2C Ⓓ 01D Ⓒ web-silver   2D Ⓓ 01D Ⓒ freemarket

3A Ⓓ Diagram   3B Ⓓ Matchstic Ⓒ Atlas Realty   3C Ⓓ UlrichPinciotti Design Group Ⓒ HCR ManorCare   3D Ⓓ R&R Partners Ⓒ Athletes For Hope

4A Ⓓ Karl Design Vienna Ⓒ Jeunesse Austria   4B Ⓓ El Creative Ⓒ Savings for Success   4C Ⓓ The Bradford Lawton Design Group Ⓒ Heart Transplant Surgery   4D Ⓓ FutureBrand Ⓒ Melbourne

5A Ⓓ 01D Ⓒ web2people   5B Ⓓ Burocratik—Design Ⓒ   5C Ⓓ BPG Design Ⓒ Imdaad   5D Ⓓ Brainding

	A	B	C	D
1				
2				
3				
4				
5				

D = Design Firm   C = Client

1A D Headshot brand development C AquaEra   1B D Pure Identity Design C Sure Shot   1C D juancazu C GNS AMERICAN EXPRESS   1D D The Bradford Lawton Design Group C San Antonio River Foundation

2A D Hemmo.nl C Clq.nl—City of Delft   2B D Emblem C Yoga Yoga   2C D logobyte   2D D Reaction Design & Printing C Desert Med Aesthetics

3A D bartodell.com C Angels   3B D For the Love of Creating C Premier Baby Concierge   3C D Diagram   3D D Denis Olenik Design Studio C Intechcore

4A D Goloubinov C Yellowmountain   4B D APSITS C Space Music   4C D Hand dizajn studio C Djecji vrtic Kastela   4D D Nynas C Luke's Locker

5A D Marlin C Mission Foodservice   5B D Gyula Németh C Human telex   5C D Squires and Company C Deep Ellum Association   5D D Schwartzrock Graphic Arts C Martinson Design

	A	B	C	D
1				
2				
3				
4				
5				

A   B   C   D

      1

      2

      3

     4

       5

ⓓ = Design Firm   ⓒ = Client

1A ⓓ Gardner Design ⓒ SeaWorld   1B ⓓ diadik ⓒ 1-2-3 International   1C ⓓ mod&co ⓒ Skills For Tomorrow   1D ⓓ Thelogoloft.com

2A ⓓ The Bradford Lawton Design Group ⓒ McKenna Foundation   2B ⓓ Curtis Sharp Design ⓒ CSI Builders   2C ⓓ BXC nicelogo.com ⓒ BXC Branding & Design   2D ⓓ Graphics & Designing Inc. ⓒ Koshidaka

3A ⓓ GSW Worldwide ⓒ St. Catherine's School   3B ⓓ Skybend ⓒ Amigos of Hondoras   3C ⓓ 01D ⓒ Russian League for the Defense of Human Dignity and Security   3D ⓓ pearpod ⓒ slave free

4A ⓓ Forthright Strategic Design ⓒ Placer Chiropractic   4B ⓓ Integrated Communications (ICLA) ⓒ Donation Services   4C ⓓ Hayes Image ⓒ Williamson Pottery   4D ⓓ Diagram

5A ⓓ Tower of Babel ⓒ Flying Fingers Transcription   5B ⓓ Mauck Groves Branding & Design ⓒ Across America 06   5C ⓓ Stiles Design ⓒ The Butler Bros.   5D ⓓ Jill Carson ⓒ Carbon Tracker

LOGO SEARCH

Keywords  **Mythology**

Type: ○ Symbol ○ Typographic ○ Combo ● All

	A	B	C	D
1				
2				
3				
4				
5				

D = Design Firm   **C** = Client

1A **D** Eli Kirk **C** LDS Speed Dating   1B **D** Squires and Company **C** AeroLynx   1C **D** Skybend **C** Sentry   1D **D** orton design **C** applied composiite tech

2A **D** Dennard, Lacey & Associates **C** Steak & Ale Tavern   2B **D** Dennard, Lacey & Associates **C** VHA   2C **D** Jerron Ames **C** Arteis   2D **D** orton design **C** centaur printing

3A **D** Wox **C** Andre Werneck   3B **D** Lilagan Pandji Design **C** Singha Puri Hotel   3C **D** Glitschka Studios **C** Upper Deck Company   3D **D** Van Cyber Design **C** SoonCorp

4A **D** Jon Flaming Design **C** SeeCreature   4B **D** Glitschka Studios **C** Street Value   4C **D** SourceMecca **C** SourceMecca   4D **D** S4LE.com **C** www.monstercan.com

5A **D** Stiles Design **C** Nice Monster   5B **D** this is nido **C** tenporium   5C **D** Oliver Russell **C** Oliver Russell   5D **D** Yaroslav Zheleznyakov **C** The mayoralty of city

	A	B	C	D
1				
2				
3				
4				
5				

Ⓓ = Design Firm   Ⓒ = Client

1A Ⓓ M. Brady Clark Design Ⓒ The Militia Group   1B Ⓓ Murillo Design, Inc. Ⓒ Murillo Design, Inc.   1C Ⓓ Greteman Group Ⓒ Sarah Jane   1D Ⓓ Kloom Ⓒ Online Performance Group

2A Ⓓ Rickabaugh Graphics Ⓒ Univ. of Central Florida   2B Ⓓ Thinkpen Design, Inc. Ⓒ Stonecrete Designs, Inc.   2C Ⓓ The Joe Bosack Graphic Design Co. Ⓒ Brewton Parker College   2D Ⓓ Velocity Design Group Ⓒ Howalt Design

3A Ⓓ VanPaul Design Ⓒ Zeus MMA   3B Ⓓ Nicole Romer Ⓒ Oui   3C Ⓓ mugur mihai Ⓒ Beachside Resort   3D Ⓓ Rob McClurkan Illustration Ⓒ The Real Bread Company

4A Ⓓ LEKKERWERKEN Ⓒ Lekkerwerken   4B Ⓓ cypher13 Ⓒ TEEBEEland   4C Ⓓ LeoDesign Ⓒ Microsoft   4D Ⓓ futska llc Ⓒ pookie

5A Ⓓ lunabrand design group Ⓒ Fairytale Brownies   5B Ⓓ orton design Ⓒ entityagency.com   5C Ⓓ 229   5D Ⓓ Glitschka Studios Ⓒ Lounja

126

Lemonades from Arbuzov
Identity and Product Design

Y-Design, Yaroslavl, Russia

Russian designer Yaroslav Zheleznyakov of Y-Design in the city of Yaroslavl, Russia, explains that his client's product—lemonade—although ubiquitous in other parts of the world, is perhaps a bit more out of the ordinary in his region.

"The client is engaged in the manufacture of lemonade in bottles and will market it under the name 'Lemonades from Arbuzov,' so the trademark translates to "lemonades from watermelons,'" Zheleznyakov says. "'Watermelons' are the invented surname of the seller of the product. The name was amusing to the client and me too."

In Russia, consumers' relationship to lemonade is different than in other places. It is never something that children would sell at a sidewalk stand, and almost never would anyone make it at home. In addition, it is usually a carbonated drink sold only in shops or cafeterias. Lemonade is regarded as a children's drink, related to holidays and nostalgia.

"But lemonade is considered to be a bit old-fashioned, purchased now by people middle-aged and older," Zheleznyakov says. The designer wanted to find a way to refresh the concept of the drink itself and make it more relevant to consumers today.

He decided to play off of the nostalgia component. Buyers in the client's target group not only thought back fondly on lemonade as a happy childhood memory, but they would also have the same feelings for the circus, which Zheleznyakov says was more popular than the movies at the time. So he started to experiment with Cyrillic lettering that would be reminiscent of a circus poster of the time. But he made the letterforms and colors very contemporary, almost like graffiti.

Through many trials, he puzzled together letterforms into a leaf shape. The result is as much an intricate illustration or illumination as it is a trademark name. Its color is easily changed to reflect the client's various flavor offerings, and it sits nicely on the clear bottles of drink.

The client was very happy with the design, the designer reports. The packaging stands out among competitors' products because it is so unusual and contrary.

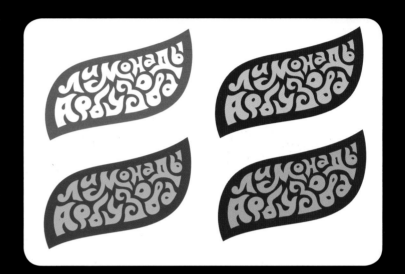

Russian designer Yaroslav Zheleznyakov wanted not only to give the product a distinctive look with his new identity, but also to refresh the way Russian's viewed lemonade.

"An impudent design which is not a standard representation of usual labels, in this case, for lemonade, has turned out well," Zheleznyakov says. "It is interesting for me to work on the project because the client was not afraid to take risks. He was not afraid to be unlike anybody else. Nonstandard and courageous decisions seldom happen in life."

	A	B	C	D
1	# LOGO SEARCH Keywords **Birds** Type: ○ Symbol ○ Typographic ○ Combo ● All			
2				
3				
4				
5				

Ⓓ = Design Firm   Ⓒ = Client

1C Ⓓ Schwartzrock Graphic Arts Ⓒ Minnesota Health and Housing Association   1D Ⓓ Squires and Company Ⓒ Chico's

2A Ⓓ Schwartzrock Graphic Arts Ⓒ Westwood Lutheran Church   2B Ⓓ Giles Design Inc. Ⓒ Victory Ranch Club   2C Ⓓ Lienhart Design Ⓒ First Federal Bank   2D Ⓓ Velocity Design Group Ⓒ Freedom Board Shop

3A Ⓓ Haven Productions Ⓒ Haven Productions—Spec Work   3B Ⓓ Stygar Group, Inc. Ⓒ The Aluminum Association   3C Ⓓ Gyula Németh Ⓒ Budapest Eagles   3D Ⓓ Rickabaugh Graphics Ⓒ IUP

4A Ⓓ McGuire Design Ⓒ Robert McGuire   4B Ⓓ orton design Ⓒ pheonix island   4C Ⓓ Tandem Design Agency Ⓒ Wilson Kester Law   4D Ⓓ Pejot Ⓒ Davidson Consulting

5A Ⓓ Murillo Design, Inc. Ⓒ Murillo Design, Inc.   5B Ⓓ Branders, Inc. Ⓒ Peace Conference   5C Ⓓ Alin Golfitescu Ⓒ mobilink pakistan   5D Ⓓ KNOWGOODER Ⓒ Holy Socks

A **B** **C** **D**

1

2

3

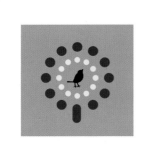

4

5

ⓓ = Design Firm   ⓒ = Client

1A ⓓ Luke Despatie & The Design Firm ⓒ The International Wild Bird Foundation 1B ⓓ Denis Olenik Design Studio ⓒ ZooSmart 1C ⓓ Glitschka Studios ⓒ Bird Fellow 1D ⓓ Gardner Design ⓒ Grace Hill Winery

2A ⓓ The Right Hand ⓒ Julia Smedovich 2B ⓓ Oxide Design Co. ⓒ Meadowlark Recycling 2C ⓓ Bryan Cooper Design ⓒ Quail Boards 2D ⓓ Ostrov Svobody ⓒ Rose Garden

3A ⓓ Allen Creative ⓒ Beachside Appraisal Group 3B ⓓ Luke Despatie & The Design Firm ⓒ The International Wild Bird Foundation 3C ⓓ guten tag! ⓒ Julie Gibson 3D ⓓ 7981Design ⓒ yuanyang Real Estate

4A ⓓ JG Creative ⓒ Boise Art museum 4B ⓓ Megan Thompson Design ⓒ Nydori 4C ⓓ Murillo Design, Inc. ⓒ Zeitgraph 4D ⓓ Loop Design ⓒ Columbia House

5A ⓓ HendrixRaderWise ⓒ HendrixRaderWise 5B ⓓ Little Jacket ⓒ Bohemian Foundation 5C ⓓ Lilagan Pandji Design ⓒ Bliss Capital 5D ⓓ Vasco Morelli Design ⓒ Sterling Vineyards

	A	B	C	D
1				
2				
3				
4				
5				

A	B	C	D	
 POULTRY FIRST				1
 watchuwant			 HAHN SLH	2
				3
				4
		LOS AMIGOS		5

Ⓓ = Design Firm   Ⓒ = Client

1A Ⓓ Roy Smith Design Ⓒ The Point/Poultry First 1B Ⓓ Pikant marketing Ⓒ Regional health organisation 1C Ⓓ Oscar Morris Ⓒ Eggers Poultry Farm 1D Ⓓ Advertising Intelligence

2A Ⓓ Chris Herron Design Ⓒ WatchuWant 2B Ⓓ demasijones Ⓒ Rosie's Australian Style Chicken 2C Ⓓ Peterson Ray & Company Ⓒ Zeus Rooster 2D Ⓓ CF Napa Brand Design Ⓒ Hahn Family Wines

3A Ⓓ Rickabaugh Graphics Ⓒ Univ. of Texas at San Antonio 3B Ⓓ Glitschka Studios Ⓒ Advanced Refrigeration & Air 3C Ⓓ Murillo Design, Inc. Ⓒ Penguin Pub 3D Ⓓ Weylon Smith Ⓒ Mike Temple

4A Ⓓ E. Tage Larsen Design Ⓒ Duckling Creative 4B Ⓓ Rob McClurkan Illustration Ⓒ Kiwi Magazine 4C Ⓓ Denis Olenik Design Studio Ⓒ ZooSmart 4D Ⓓ Offbeat Design Ⓒ World Healing Circles

5A Ⓓ 5Seven Ⓒ The Gap 5B Ⓓ Hutner Group Ⓒ Hutner Group 5C Ⓓ mod&co Ⓒ Los Amigos 5D Ⓓ Art Craft Printers & Design Ⓒ Feather Your Nest Home Interiors Boutique

LOGO SEARCH

Keywords  **Fish, Bugs, Reptiles**

Type: ○ Symbol ○ Typographic ○ Combo ● All

CAVIAR BAR
NINJA AKASAKA

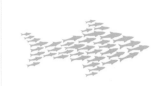

smallfish

THE GRANDER

SQUARED EYE

OLYMPIA
THE GRILL AT PIER 21

Signal Shark

Ⓓ = Design Firm   Ⓒ = Client

1C Ⓓ Graphics & Designing Inc. Ⓒ MTK   1D Ⓓ Squires and Company Ⓒ XTO Energy

2A Ⓓ Bryan Cooper Design Ⓒ Dark Shades Inc.   2B Ⓓ Studio Simon Ⓒ Toledo Walleye   2C Ⓓ Patten ID Ⓒ MRG   2D Ⓓ POLLARDdesign Ⓒ Aqua Scent

3A Ⓓ Quentin Duncan   3B Ⓓ R&R Partners Ⓒ Personal   3C Ⓓ 7981Design Ⓒ haiyuerestaurant   3D Ⓓ High Tide Creative Ⓒ The Grander

4A Ⓓ APSITS Ⓒ MTV UK   4B Ⓓ Creative NRG Ⓒ Aquatics Unlimited   4C Ⓓ KTD Ⓒ Lone Star Aquaria   4D Ⓓ Able Ⓒ Squared Eye

5A Ⓓ Judson Design Ⓒ Olympia Grill   5B Ⓓ Diagram   5C Ⓓ Reactive Mediums Ⓒ Chris Green   5D Ⓓ Felixsockwell.com Ⓒ the fin 3

A	B	C	D	
		 OCTOPUS SUSHI BAR		1
 RentHouse		 AQUANAUT		2
				3
			 Rentzilla	4
 KAMÉLIO	 leap			5

	A	B	C	D
1	 **monarch** CONSULTING	 ALEGRÍA ~COSTA RICA~	 BUTTERFLY BAY kahikatoa	
2	 JINAIR	 RHETT MILLER		 FIREFLY
3			 dustyb	 ƎƁEE three bee creative studios
4	 SUPERFLY	 SUPERFLY	 Super Fly	 Mr$crooge Your online wiser miser.
5				

Ⓓ = Design Firm   Ⓒ = Client

1A Ⓓ ellen bruss design Ⓒ Monarch   1B Ⓓ Hero Design Studio Ⓒ Tandem Brand   1C Ⓓ Indigo Creative Ⓒ Butterfly Bay   1D Ⓓ Ad Impact Advertising Ⓒ Worldwide Online Printing

2A Ⓓ FutureBrand Ⓒ Korean Air   2B Ⓓ josh higgins design Ⓒ Rhett Miller   2C Ⓓ Gardner Design Ⓒ Lavish Boutique   2D Ⓓ Opolis Design, LLC Ⓒ Firefly

3A Ⓓ Gardner Design Ⓒ Collins Bus   3B Ⓓ Hirschmann Design Ⓒ Jim & Nick's Bar-B-Q   3C Ⓓ Brainding Ⓒ Dusty B   3D Ⓓ julian peck Ⓒ 3BEE Creative Studio

4A Ⓓ Karl Design Vienna Ⓒ Spirit / Superfly Radio GmbH   4B Ⓓ Karl Design Vienna Ⓒ Spirit / Superfly Radio GmbH   4C Ⓓ Karl Design Vienna Ⓒ Spirit / Superfly Radio GmbH   4D Ⓓ Chris Rooney Illustration/Design Ⓒ Mr. Scrooge

5A Ⓓ Gardner Design Ⓒ Grace Hill Winery   5B Ⓓ Logoholik Ⓒ globalroach.com   5C Ⓓ 01D Ⓒ Ufakalyan.ru   5D Ⓓ LogoDesignGuru.com

Collins Bus
Logo Design

Gardner Design, Wichita, Kansas

The new identity for Collins Bus, created by Gardner Design, includes a rear-view-mirror-like logo and a word mark that mimics the shape and length of a Class A bus.

Can a logo be forward-facing while looking backward? In the case of a new mark created by Gardner Design for Collins Bus, the answer is "yes."

Collins produces Class A school buses. It already owned Mid Bus and purchased competitor Corbeil 2008. To meld the three companies and to announce Collins' new status, a new identity was needed.

School buses are largely commodity products. Although they are built from the chassis up according to the customer's specific needs (each school district has very different requirements, such as having safety belts or not), the vehicles are largely the same. Some customers might be more loyal to one supplier or another, but usually school districts place orders according to a company's ability to meet a delivery date or an already established budget.

Another challenge: Some school districts allow Collins to place its logo on buses, while others only permit the word mark or nothing at all. So the finished design would have to be conservative enough to be acceptable to most bus customers to increase the chances that it could be used at all.

The team at Gardner Design believed that the new identity presented an opportunity to not only boost Collins' visibility in the market, but also create a more resonant, emotional tie with the client's ultimate customer—the bus driver. After all, that's the person who eventually reports back to the school board on whether they liked that product or not. The Collins' brand needed to be foremost in their minds.

Designer Luke Bott developed two distinct directions. One took the shape of a bus and turned it into a bee. The yellow-and-black color scheme worked for both objects, and buses and bees are both very busy things. The design had plenty of personality and was certainly memorable.

But the direction that emerged as strongest was a concept that presented the view a driver would see from a buses' side mirror. "It's looking at the identity from the driver's perspective," says Bott. "You are looking back, looking out for something. It speaks of safety. The driver is charged with the safety of the children: The mirror provides that."

He experimented with different mirror shapes and the distorted views a convex mirror would provide, but an oval mirror that reflected the stripes as they recede away from the viewer worked on another level: The mirror bends the familiar stripes into the letter C, for Collins (and, coincidentally, Corbeil). The shape of a road winding away into the horizon is another tight conceptual tie. Light sheets off the logo, just as it would off the side of a bus.

The counters in the letters for word mark Collins picks up on the window and door window shapes of a bus, points out firm principal Bill Gardner: A cross section of the top of the *O* also mimics the shape of the top of a bus. "The name sits well by itself if it needs to," he adds.

LOGO SEARCH

Keywords **Animals**

Type: ○ Symbol ○ Typographic ○ Combo ● All

	A	B	C	D
1				
2				
3				
4				
5				

Ⓓ = Design Firm   Ⓒ = Client

	A	B	C	D
1				
2				
3				
4				
5				

	A	B	C	D
1				
2				
3			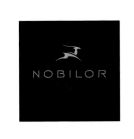	
4				
5				

	A	B	C	D
1				
2				
3				
4				
5				

A	B	C	D	
				1
				2
				3
				4
				5

Ⓓ = Design Firm   Ⓒ = Client

1A Ⓓ Brains on Fire Ⓒ New South Construction Supply   1B Ⓓ The Joe Bosack Graphic Design Co. Ⓒ Charlotte Checkers   1C Ⓓ Carrihan Creative Group Ⓒ BearNotes   1D Ⓓ Ulyanov Denis Ⓒ ZooPack

2A Ⓓ Squires and Company Ⓒ Panda Energy   2B Ⓓ Opolis Design, LLC Ⓒ Tropolis   2C Ⓓ Glitschka Studios Ⓒ Advanced Refrigeration & Air   2D Ⓓ The Joe Bosack Graphic Design Co. Ⓒ Charlotte Checkers

3A Ⓓ Creative Beard Ⓒ Culture Pop Clothing   3B Ⓓ Gee + Chung Design Ⓒ DCM   3C Ⓓ Todd Linkner Design Associates Ⓒ Viking Studios   3D Ⓓ Levy Innovations Ⓒ Manitowoc Bandits

4A Ⓓ Gardner Design Ⓒ ParkStone   4B Ⓓ Darkstone&Cardinal Ⓒ Illusion Studio   4C Ⓓ L*U*K*E Ⓒ Blue Tractor Cook Shop   4D Ⓓ Gardner Design Ⓒ Grace Hill Winery

5A Ⓓ ForeScene & Your Eyes Here Ⓒ unused—spec work ForeScene   5B Ⓓ Tomsuey Inc. Ⓒ Coogee Imports LLC   5C Ⓓ Studio Simon Ⓒ SUNY Canton   5D Ⓓ soViet Ⓒ Wealth Smart

Ⓓ = Design Firm Ⓒ = Client

1A Ⓓ www.zka11.com 1B Ⓓ this is nido Ⓒ elephruit 1C Ⓓ Spela Draslar Ⓒ Urska Smolej, s.p. 1D Ⓓ jing Ⓒ Lee Silsby Pharmacy

2A Ⓓ Sayles Graphic Design, Inc. Ⓒ Big Ass Pack 2B Ⓓ vladimir sijerkovic Ⓒ Istocna Cuda—Eastern Miracles 2C Ⓓ Murillo Design, Inc. Ⓒ Murillo Design, Inc. 2D Ⓓ The Robin Shepherd Group Ⓒ The Jacksonville Zoo

3A Ⓓ Burn Creative Ⓒ Laing Group 3B Ⓓ Jovan Rocanov Ⓒ Rhino Design Group 3C Ⓓ Chris Corneal Ⓒ Symbiotic Solutions 3D Ⓓ The Bradford Lawton Design Group Ⓒ San Antonio Zoo

4A Ⓓ Patten ID Ⓒ Monkeywise Marketing 4B Ⓓ bartodell.com Ⓒ Escape Custom Audio 4C Ⓓ tarsha hall design Ⓒ Natale Design Ⓒ Starving Monkey Productions LLC

5A Ⓓ PaperSky Design Ⓒ Catering Productions 5B Ⓓ Schwartzrock Graphic Arts Ⓒ Design Center, Inc. 5C Ⓓ Small Dog Design Ⓒ Ear Nose Throat Ballarat 5D Ⓓ Sussner Design Company Ⓒ animal humane society

Shaun Saxon
Logo Design

Roy Smith, Norwich, England

(Left) The finished identity for Shaun Saxon Photography is elegant, refined, and certainly memorable.

(Below) Designer Roy Smith experimented with photographic and wedding imagery before deciding on the symbol for infinity, which was appropriate for both categories.

When Shaun Saxon, a Florida photographer who specializes in custom fine art portraits and documentary wedding photography, decided he needed an identity for his studio, he wanted to communicate the messages of "high end," "expensive," and "value added." But he also wanted to get across the nature of his product: dramatic, dreamy, natural photography with a creative and edgy fashion feel.

One additional requirement: Like many photographers, he needed to use all or part of the new logo to brand his Web-based display photos so that they could not be reproduced without permission. This meant that the new logo should be solid and recognizable enough to be printed onto the photo margin, like a personal signature.

Designer Roy Smith was contacted by Saxon through a website that showcases designers' work. After learning what Saxon wanted, Smith began the project by assembling a mood board of various photographers' logos and images that were related to photographic paraphernalia and engagement, wedding, and portrait photography. There was a definite trend toward script signatures and initial monograms. Classic serifs and fine sans fonts were also commonplace. Photographic icons, however, were rarely used well.

While he believes a successful logo should communicate its message simply and effectively, Smith doesn't think it is necessary for everything to be taken in on the first viewing. He endeavors to introduce an element of intrigue into his identity work to keep it memorable and fresh.

He began to make a series of thumbnail sketches in pen, drawing various camera features such as the aperture, tripod, and symbols

found on a camera. Celtic knots, calligraphic scrolls, and matrimonial paraphernalia were also explored in these drawings.

"The infinity loop seemed the obvious way forward since it appears on the camera lens itself and is also a widely recognized symbol for eternity and everlasting love—perfect for an engagement, wedding, and portrait photographer," Smith says. "The challenge was to use it in a way never seen before."

Smith achieved that by weaving the symbol itself into the word "Saxon," deftly replacing the *a*, *x*, and *o*. The combination produced a word mark that also housed the logo. It also created the proprietary mark that the photographer needed for branding his photos (and, eventually, to be used as a watermark for stationery).

LOGO SEARCH

Keywords **Nature**

Type: ○ Symbol ○ Typographic ○ Combo ⦿ All

	A	B	C	D
1				
2		 Red Leaf	 THREE PATHS	
3	 cha Colorado Hospital Association	 EXCLUSIVE RESORTS	 reverence	
4		 BROADLEAF		green Orchid
5	 vipassana Hawaiʻi		 Thornhill INTERIORS	 acoustigreen

	A	B	C	D
1		 SILVERTHORNE	 THORNTON·PLACE NORTHGATE	 FruitaBü ORGANIC SMOOOSHED FRUIT
2	 ORGANICALLY HAPPY	 BAILEY NURSERIES	 ASHWOOD	 Kashi The Seven Whole Grain Company
3	 Natura			
4			 Path with Art	
5	 nektar	 كلية القـدس ALQUDS COLLEGE	 STONEFIELD	 BLOESEM

	A	B	C	D

A1  lotus

B1  origins — EXOTIC VARIETAL TREATS

C1  HUMAN CAPITAL INSTITUTE

D1 SOMA AUSTRALIA  — 1

A2  PARK ANGELS

B2  BOUQUETS FOR BOOKS

C2  STACEY AMBROSIO photography

D2  — 2

A3  Urbivore {urban nature}

B3

C3  Wildwood Canyon ~ Inn at Telluride

D3 BIGMOUNTAIN — 3

A4  shareyourwishes

B4  IN MEMORIAM

C4  ECOJOY • HAPPY SOIL • HAPPY PLANTS •

D4  GREENSTREET — 4

A5

B5  Sappy CARDS

C5  OLD VILLAGE OLIVE OIL | HUILE D'OLIVE

D5  fresh start — 5

Ⓓ = Design Firm   Ⓒ = Client

	A	B	C	D
1	 The Giving Tree	 consultants in CARDIOLOGY	 STAR OAK PROPERTIES	
2	 THE MAILBOX CLUB		 threeheads	 TREEmendous
3		 Núcleo de Projetos	 greenthumb PROJECT	 GREENTHUMB ARCHITECTURE
4		 MID-IOWA HEALTH FOUNDATION	 FOReST METAL GROUP	
5	 Caliope's Cottage	 orangetreeproject		 ARBORETUM

A   B   C   D

1

2

3

4

5

D = Design Firm   C = Client

1A D ArtFly C Casa Verde Custom Homes   1B D T&E Polydorou Design Ltd C InterContinental Aphrodite Hills Resort Hotel Cyprus   1C D Dennard, Lacey & Associates C Sweet Oak Hunting Club
1D D The Robin Shepherd Group C Centex Homes   2A D FUEL Creative Group C McClone Construction Company   2B D 2B Design C Plant Healthcare, Inc.   2C D Diagram   2D D La Visual C Tree Tea
3A D Phony Lawn C Monteverdi   3B D Peak Seven C Diamond Falls Estates   3C D Design Army C World Bank   3D D Christian Palino Design C Kinfo
4A D The Bradford Lawton Design Group C La Arcata Retail Center   4B D themarsdesign.net C Pardee Homes   4C D Schwartzrock Graphic Arts C Design Center, Inc.   4D D Tower of Babel C Western Rivers Conservancy
5A D beau bureau Kommunikationsdesign C swissmade: Unique things from Switzerland   5B D MSI C Kmart   5C D MSI C Kmart   5D D pearpod C learn to ski for good

149

	A	B	C	D

A **B** **C** **D**

1

EMEA GOLD CLUB
TENERIFE - CANARY ISLANDS

Blu Water
day spa. nails. boutique

BLUE POINTE
PLASTICS

2

MUTUAL PARK
CAPITAL

Lachome
IMMOBILIARE

NORTHERN
COLORADO
OUTDOORS

3

Oxigeno Arquitectura

the wild sea

TWIN RIVERS

sky blue
marketing

4

CREMA
CAFE

HARMONY
OUTDOOR LIVING CENTER

BuySAFE

5

CLUBLIFE

rebrewal

Ⓓ = Design Firm Ⓒ = Client

1A Ⓓ Carlson Marketing Worldwide Ⓒ microsoft 1B Ⓓ Wantulok Design Ⓒ Blu Water 1C Ⓓ Jerron Ames Ⓒ Arteis 1D Ⓓ Hemmo.nl Ⓒ Clq.nl—AM Wonen

2A Ⓓ Hula+Hula Ⓒ Kong 2B Ⓓ Pink Tank Creative Ⓒ Mutual Park Capital 2C Ⓓ Cacao Design Ⓒ Lachome 2D Ⓓ D&Dre Creative Ⓒ blackwhite conspiracy

3A Ⓓ Sol Consultores Ⓒ Oxigeno Arquitectura 3B Ⓓ Alphabet Arm Design Ⓒ Todd Russell 3C Ⓓ The Brand Agency Ⓒ Peet Limited 3D Ⓓ GingerBee Creative

4A Ⓓ Cricket Design Works Ⓒ Creme Cafe 4B Ⓓ Periscope Ⓒ Harmony Outdoor Living Center 4C Ⓓ Steve Cantrell Ⓒ Tanergy 4D Ⓓ Opolis Design, LLC Ⓒ BuySafe

5A Ⓓ Ginter & Miletina Ⓒ Heliodor 5B Ⓓ Mindgruve Ⓒ ClubLife 5C Ⓓ mod&co Ⓒ Calhoun Square 5D Ⓓ King Design Office Ⓒ Sustainable Energy Partners

150

Jack in the Box
Identity Design

Duffy & Partners, Minneapolis, Minnesota

One of the more oddly charming fast-food spokes-characters to emerge from the crowd of kings, clowns, dogs, and other undefined mammals in the past decade is Jack, the round-headed, business-suited character who fronts for Jack in the Box restaurants.

Created in 1995 by Chiat/Day/Secret Weapon, Jack has become the very visible "head" of the 2,100-plus chain of stores, which are located primarily in the western United States (the first of which opened in 1951). His incongruous head and attire, combined with his take-charge attitude, is quirky and forceful. He is large (-headed) and in charge. He has the customer's best interests in mind always.

"Jack has become the personality of the chain—it's all Jack," says Joe Duffy, principal of Duffy & Partners, the Minneapolis-based design firm who was invited to create a new brand identity that matched Jack in verve and quirk. "He watches over everything and makes sure the customer gets what he wants. Customers have developed a real thing for Jack."

At the time Duffy's team began work on the project, the chain's existing identity was somewhat spiritless. The logo was composed of fat, tubular, all caps letters, some of which were conjoined in rather awkward ways. The new identity needed to have the same warmth as Jack—in other words, more human and humorous. The client asked that the brand's original red color be retained, but everything else could be changed.

The Duffy team's solution wrapped the word "Jack" around a 3-D-like box, stressing the brand's key word. Set in a customized script, in uppercase and lowercase, the name almost looks like a signature—certainly appropriate for a brand that is based entirely on an actual character. The logo is essentially his signature and stamp of approval.

"The type we chose lends itself to the format for the icon. The name box has its simple straightforward design and is also a nice complement to the Jack script. The script is more free-flowing, and the type below reigns that in a bit," Duffy explains.

The outline of the box shape creates a proprietary mark for Jack in the Box, one that can be repurposed in other ways—as a container for graphics or other type, for instance. It is also repeated to create large and small graphic patterns that will be used for packaging, POS, signage, advertising, and corporate communications.

"The Jack in the Box restaurants offer a higher quality product and a broader range of menu items—you can have what you want," says Duffy. "Everything about the restaurant needs to be of a higher quality. This is a successful brand that needed revitalization. The last thing you want to do is pull the rug out from under the client's loyal following. This identity is all about Jack and the affinity customers have for him."

The new Jack in the Box logo, designed by Duffy & Partners, was created to be the signature of the now iconic "head" of the chain, Jack. In addition, the box shape that contains the signature is endlessly repurposable, as shown here in new icons and patterning.

LOGO SEARCH

Keywords | **Shapes** |

Type: ◯ Symbol ◯ Typographic ◯ Combo ⦿ All

Κεντρική
Ασφαλιστική

Global Startups

Metronet®

академия синергии

42SBS
Solutions Business Science

Frontier Renewal

INSTYTUT
ZDROWIA I URODY

jord

INTERNATIONAL
FILTER
SOLUTIONS

SKY Q

Head Count

solergy

OPTIMUM
HEALTH

WIT-TECH

	A	B	C	D	
		GUEVARA'S MEXICAN IMPORTS	FOLK		1
					2
	HINSEGIN DAGAR Í REYKJAVÍK GAY PRIDE	Vascular Center of Northern Michigan	SunRise 2008		3
		RAYV	Jehiah		4
			TREND		5

Ⓓ = Design Firm Ⓒ = Client

1A Ⓓ Triple Frog LLC Ⓒ Sue Hartt 1B Ⓓ bartodell.com Ⓒ Guevara's Mexican Imports 1C Ⓓ Ozidea Ⓒ Ukrainian Social Network 1D Ⓓ El Paso, Galeria de Comunicacion Ⓒ Universidad Carlos III de Madrid
2A Ⓓ Dessein Ⓒ Vanguard Investments 2B Ⓓ b_werk markenarchitektur gmbh Ⓒ Optimal Foto 2C Ⓓ Martin Jordan Ⓒ Ministry of Education, Youth and Sports Brandenburg 2D Ⓓ Gardner Design Ⓒ Pulse Systems Inc.
3A Ⓓ Fiton Ⓒ n/a 3B Ⓓ Tandem Design Agency Ⓒ Vascular Center of Northern Michigan 3C Ⓓ Carlson Marketing Worldwide Ⓒ Sun Microsystems 3D Ⓓ TypeOrange Ⓒ TypeOrange
4A Ⓓ Canvas Astronauts & Agriculture Ⓒ Coenco Group 4B Ⓓ MSDS Ⓒ RayV 4C Ⓓ 38one Ⓒ Jehiah Czebotar 4D Ⓓ Paul Jobson Ⓒ onesummer design
5A Ⓓ Ramp Ⓒ Denimhead 5B Ⓓ Pawel Tomas "Substrate" Ⓒ Pilz 5C Ⓓ 5 Fifteen Design Group, Inc. Ⓒ Trend Graphics 5D Ⓓ Obnocktious Ⓒ Michael & Susan Dell Foundation

	A	B	C	D
1	 Optimum online	 cpod®	 HIDROSOPH	
2	 EUROPA	 ENK INVEST	 Sync	
3	 DMÍ	 elroy systems INCORPORATED	 response group	
4		 INTRE	 sunlink	 soliya™
5	 mosaic GLOBAL SOLUTIONS	 Atlas Strategies	 COMPLIANCE・ETHICS	inviragen

	A	B	C	D
1				
2				
3				
4				
5				

1A Ⓓ Chris Rooney Illustration/Design Ⓒ San Francisco Film Society 1B Ⓓ PULK Ⓒ Virgin Records 1C Ⓓ Skin Designstudio Ⓒ Afontibus 1D Ⓓ Gardner Design Ⓒ Cessna Service Centers

2A Ⓓ The Brand Agency Ⓒ LandCorp 2B Ⓓ Timber Design Company Ⓒ Third Eye Records & Management 2C Ⓓ Kloom Ⓒ Cecash 2D Ⓓ Squires and Company Ⓒ Chico's

3A Ⓓ Gardner Design Ⓒ Kansas Heart Hospital 3B Ⓓ Bounce Design Newcastle Pty Ltd Ⓒ New Lake 3C Ⓓ Spoonbend Ⓒ Citrine 3D Ⓓ Phony Lawn Ⓒ Epic Day

4A Ⓓ Gardner Design Ⓒ Datility 4B Ⓓ Gardner Design Ⓒ C Financial 4C Ⓓ Seamer Design Ⓒ Motek 4D Ⓓ A3 Design Ⓒ Medical University of South Carolina

5A Ⓓ Gardner Design Ⓒ Clipper Capital 5B Ⓓ Gardner Design Ⓒ Clipper Capital 5C Ⓓ 903 Creative, LLC Ⓒ Buggs Island Telephone 5D Ⓓ Gardner Design Ⓒ Clipper Capital

	A	B	C	D
1				
2				
3				
4				
5				

D = Design Firm **C** = Client

| A | B | C | D |

1

2

3

4

5

	A	B	C	D
1	 paradigm	LLOYD GROUP	SUPRA	ICONIK
2	APOKA	breathing easier a comprehensive survey of asthma treatment options	IGNITE ELITE ATHLETIC TRAINING	
3		SPORT GARDEN Warsaw Sport Complex		UMW
4				
5		CRT	XBITECH	

Ⓓ = Design Firm   Ⓒ = Client

1A Ⓓ themarsdesign.net Ⓒ Paradigm   1B Ⓓ Phixative Ⓒ LLoyd Group   1C Ⓓ San Markos Ⓒ supra   1D Ⓓ The Mixx Ⓒ Iconik

2A Ⓓ APOKA Ⓒ APOKA   2B Ⓓ Flywheel Design Ⓒ strategic pharma   2C Ⓓ Vigor—interactive branding strategy Ⓒ Ignite   2D Ⓓ Valhalla | Design & Conquer Ⓒ Adio Shoes

3A Ⓓ Range Ⓒ City of Dallas—The Trinity River Corridor   3B Ⓓ Diagram   3C Ⓓ Gardner Design Ⓒ Cessna Service Centers   3D Ⓓ Lippincott Ⓒ UMW

4A Ⓓ Gardner Design Ⓒ C Financial   4B Ⓓ Gardner Design Ⓒ BiTemp   4C Ⓓ Gardner Design Ⓒ BiTemp   4D Ⓓ 01D Ⓒ Aluplast

5A Ⓓ Team Y&R Ⓒ Arabian Properties   5B Ⓓ TPG Architecture Ⓒ CRT   5C Ⓓ Brainding Ⓒ XBitech   5D Ⓓ metaforma design Ⓒ metaforma design

	A	B	C	D
1			 LEXPRO экспертная юридическая система	
2			 COSTA LADERA	
3	 OPEN SQUARE FOUNDATION	 TowerGroup TOMORROW'S ADVANTAGE. TODAY.	 PEOPLE FILTER	 DEPOSIT ALTERNATIVE
4	 LACPS LOS ANGELES CENTER FOR PHOTOGRAPHIC STUDIES	 chfa	 SCHIFF BAUER GASSE	 QL2
5		 LTC	 JOT IT	ADISTA

Ⓓ = Design Firm Ⓒ = Client

	A	B	C	D
1		 KASTMÜLLER		
2		 ohms		RAVI 
3	 jaltex	 Instyll		 waldrons solicitors
4	 NIAGARA FALLS HYDRO	 Musica	 vitæ	
5			 IIS Benefits	 the Archive

A	B	C	D	
		 SKYCOURTS DUBAILAND		1
 FRENCH PROPERTY EXHIBITION	 GRAND PIAZZA CHICAGO	 JAWA		2
	 MARCO VITELLI	 Security Industry Awards	 windesal	3
 MERIDIAN Luxury Apartments AT THE CROSSING	 VANTAGE	 zeledyne	 AmeriCompass	4
 en veer	 XOMA	 GCAA		5

Identity Design

Landor Associates, Hamburg, Germany

INTERPIPE

Before its brand relaunch, almost everything about Interpipe sounded gray, dark, and metallic. A leading manufacturer of steel pipe and wheels in the emerging Eastern European region of Ukraine, it had an identity that spoke dimly of its origins during the Communist era.

But the identity it carries today, courtesy of the Landor Associates' office in Hamburg, Germany, provides a much different experience. Dominated by yellow, its logo and accompanying system are solid, bright, and definitely part of the larger twenty-first century world.

When it began working with Landor in 2006, Interpipe wanted to leave behind the negative, old-fashioned image from its past and connect with the larger, transparent world of Western-oriented economies. Its management wanted to portray values of modern global corporations that reflect public interest, reliability, and security in the steel industry and become a strong employer brand of choice.

The brand and logo design that Landor produced sprang from the essence of the business itself: its products.

"The design reminds you of pipes or wheels as they interact when they are stacked together. We materialized the passive gap between the round-shaped products," says creative director Alexander Schönfeld.

These negative spaces—played out in white against vibrant yellow circles—represent the human part of the company, the branding expert explains. These are the employees and customers, with their energy, ideas, and services. (Some also see the capital letter I for Interpipe in the white shape.)

Blue (for sky) and yellow (for agriculture) are the national colors of the Ukraine. So the use of yellow was an important link to the company's origins as it became a worldwide organization. But it was not intended to be purely nation-centric. Instead, the warm, energetic yellow was a real point of differentiation in Interpipe's field of competitors, in which most use blue, gray, or other cool colors in their identities.

The designers selected and customized Daxline Pro for the Interpipe word mark. It is bold and sturdy, a necessary support and stable foundation for the logo that sits above it. The letterforms have been rounded slightly to emphasize the round shapes in the logo. The face was also chosen because it had a good Cyrillic cut, still a rarity even today, Schönfeld says.

The photography used as part of the system is redolent with images from nature. These form an excellent foil against which to consider the client's heavy, metallic product.

Ever since the new identity was put into motion, Landor has also been working with the client's employees to help them learn to "speak and live" the brand.

The trade show display and printed piece demonstrate how the use of yellow, natural images, and plenty of white space modernizes and humanizes Interpipe's very heavy, metallic, and gray products.

LOGO SEARCH

Keywords  **Symbols**

Type: ○ Symbol ○ Typographic ○ Combo ● All

A B C D

1

2   

FISHING TEXAS LAKES

3   HeadCountAsia

4

КРЕМЛЬ МЕДИА

5

retrospreads

	A	B	C	D
1			 cardiologic	 KARDIA
2		 pathos		
3				
4				
5				

1

2

3

4

5

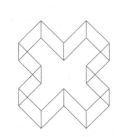

	A	B	C	D
1		SOUTH DAVIS COMMUNITY HOSPITAL		
2		Geneva Communications		{ INSIDE : OUT TECHNOLOGY }
3		BEYOND BOUNDARIES		
4	slingbeat	Chwastyka	Books Alive	TimelyReader™
5		SKÁLDSAGNA KLÚBBURINN	book club	

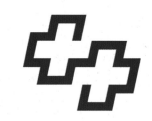

Ⓓ = Design Firm Ⓒ = Client

1A Ⓓ 3 Advertising LLC Ⓒ MERP 1B Ⓓ Fluid Studio Ⓒ South Davis Community Hospital 1C Ⓓ Just Creative Design Ⓒ Square Room 1D Ⓓ Shawn Huff Ⓒ Robert LaBaw
2A Ⓓ Beveridge Seay, Inc. Ⓒ Lifelink, M.D. 2B Ⓓ Pawel Tomas "Substrate" Ⓒ Geneva Communications 2C Ⓓ Entropy Brands Ⓒ Avalaunch Festival 2D Ⓓ co:lab Ⓒ Motorola
3A Ⓓ Squires and Company Ⓒ Distribution Management Corporation 3B Ⓓ Schwartzrock Graphic Arts Ⓒ BI 3C Ⓓ Integrated Media, Inc. Ⓒ Omnisource Marketing Group 3D Ⓓ Fiton Ⓒ Iceland Express
4A Ⓓ Alphabet Arm Design Ⓒ SlingBeat Media, LLC 4B Ⓓ Diagram 4C Ⓓ The Robin Shepherd Group Ⓒ The Jacksonville Film Festival 4D Ⓓ Steve Cantrell Ⓒ Timely Reader
5A Ⓓ Hirschmann Design Ⓒ Barnes & Noble 5B Ⓓ Hvita husid Ⓒ Mal og Menning / Edda 5C Ⓓ Big Communications Ⓒ Books-A-Million 5D Ⓓ Gardner Design Ⓒ Books for Life

Theo Chocolate
Logo and Package Design

KittenChops, Seattle, Washington

Lush, sweet, full of paint, long eyelashes, and most of all, emotion—that's what Marta Windeisen's work is. Windeisen, a.k.a. Zaara, creates both design and illustration work in her Seattle studio, KittenChops. Like a cupid's dart, her art shoots a direct connection to the reader through its simple yet sophisticated style.

The logo and packaging she created for Theo is no exception. Theo is a very high-end line of chocolate produced by Windeisen's client, Theo Chocolate. Its product flavors include such delicacies as Saffron Caramel, Burnt Sugar Ganache, Lavender Jalapeño Caramel, and Licorice Ganache.

"The whole concept of the client is that it is actually a factory—they do everything to produce the chocolate from scratch, like roast the beans, add only organic ingredients, and more to make the product, from beginning to end. There are only a few producers like this in the U.S.," Windeisen says.

The name *Theo* comes from "Theo Broma," which means "food of the gods." The name had immediate appeal to the artists: "It's short and easy to remember," she says. "It's spiritual and deeply rooted in tradition."

The client asked Windeisen to completely steer clear of two design approaches that are common to the chocolate industry: first, an old-world, European look, and second, anything that spoke of the farming of chocolate. This would include images of growers, hands lovingly holding beans, or any other literal, Wiki-like explanation.

Instead, the client wanted a logo that suggested the care and heart that goes into producing its products, but a design that was much simpler and direct than designs that were already on the market.

"It had to embrace the chocolate-making process, and it also needed to show that this is a very high-end, delicious product," the designer explains.

Her first trials explored the geographic origins of the chocolate for each variety. She experimented with collages of original folk art motives and patterns. Some designs contained images of mountains or other bits of topography. Even though all of these experiments were quite abstract, when she shared these with a focus group, Windeisen discovered that this approach was still too literal.

So she picked up a sumi brush for the word mark and oil pastels for the background and went even more abstract. After many hours of loose hand lettering with the brush, she created the final Theo logo. It's clearly a work of the human hand, less calligraphy than lovely handwriting. The addition of the cacao bean inserts the illustrative touch she loves.

Because of the weight of the logo's lines, it works well on a variety of backgrounds. For the existing product line, the colors on the packaging refer to the ingredients and their origin through color: Windeisen's oil pastel designs are like paintings. Each is unique, a treat to look at as well as eat.

"I loved this project so much that I couldn't even sleep at night. I just immersed myself in it," she says. "I like to capture the soul of what the client wants so that the design operates on an emotional level, as opposed to a 'rules level' for corporate design. Every job must bring out that soul."

LOGO SEARCH

Keywords **Arts**

Type: ◯ Symbol ◯ Typographic ◯ Combo ⦿ All

A	B	C	D

1

2

3

4

5

	A	B	C	D
1				
2				
3				
4				
5				

ⅅ = Design Firm   ⅭClient

LOGO SEARCH

Keywords | **Miscellaneous**

Type: ○ Symbol ○ Typographic ○ Combo ● All

deux ailes, un ange

PINK PASSION

great skate

Ⓓ = Design Firm   Ⓒ = Client

1C Ⓓ cogu design Ⓒ Yvonne Coutinho 1D Ⓓ IF marketing & advertising Ⓒ North Cypress Medical Center

2A Ⓓ The Eppstein Group Ⓒ Judge McCoy 2B Ⓓ Roman Kotikov Ⓒ King office 2C Ⓓ ex nihilo Ⓒ 2 ailes un ange 2D Ⓓ La Visual Ⓒ Rain Master, Inc

3A Ⓓ Richards Brock Miller Mitchell & Associates Ⓒ Lantea Group 3B Ⓓ Ulyanov Denis Ⓒ National Shoe Company 3C Ⓓ The Martin Group Ⓒ Great Skate 3D Ⓓ NOT A CANNED HAM Ⓒ Canadian Football League

4A Ⓓ Karl Design Vienna Ⓒ Texas Water Association 4B Ⓓ Tim Frame Design Ⓒ Touristees.com 4C Ⓓ Dotzero Design Ⓒ King's Coffee & Tea 4D Ⓓ Chris Rooney Illustration/Design Ⓒ Foster Farms

5A Ⓓ M. Brady Clark Design Ⓒ Personal ID 5B Ⓓ R Design LLC Ⓒ Third Party Insight 5C Ⓓ For the Love of Creating Ⓒ Tiffiney Photography 5D Ⓓ Shawn Huff Ⓒ P. Jay Massey—cocodesign.com

	A	B	C	D
1		 take **FOUR**		 MOBILE **PATROL**
2			THE LAUNCH CREW 	
3				
4		 DIGILOCK®	 autonomous women's house zagreb	 ΠΟΣΕΙΔΟΝΙΑ SEAFOOD & SEADRINKS
5		 RED WHEELBARROW PERSONAL GARDENING + LANDSCAPE CARE		

Floresta da Lua
Logo Design

C2, Portugal

When you know that the client for the Portuguese design firm C2's Floresta da Lua project requested that the elements of a moon and a tree be included in its new logo design, the final design—on the surface—doesn't seem that surprising. But art director Rui Chasqueira reveals that there is much more to the design: Its simplicity belies its complexity.

Floresta da Lua ("Moon Forest") is a Portuguese company that provides products and services in agroforestry. It serves private farm owners and institutional groups from its base in the historic Sintra Mountain in western Portugal. During the times of Roman occupation, the range was called "the moon's mountains."

The biggest challenge for any logo design, Chasqueira says, is to make a brand simple but to synthesize it in a way so it communicates not only its meaning but the values of the company. A key value of Floresta da Lua in its service to customers is an abiding concern for every single tree.

The name of the company and the client's demands were specific, so the C2 team began their design explorations by looking for ways to combine the concept of tree and moon.

"We studied the use of several trees to communicate the forest element, inserting the moon among these elements or even applying the moon as a background for the trees. But we didn't follow this line because it made the logo designs too heavy in information. When the moon was applied on the background, it made the brand look nocturnal, bringing a shady and negative appearance to the brand," he says.

They decided that using a single tree as a symbol would have much more impact. They selected the oak, a tree that is native to the area. With a shorter trunk and wide top, the tree had a distinct shape. The designers' first explorations involved forming leaves in the shape of moons. They were pleased with the overall approach, but the shape of the leaves became indistinct when the logo was used in smaller sizes.

"The moon was the principal degree of difference for the brand [among other agroforestry companies]," Chasqueira explains.

They decided to invert the concept, this time focusing on the shape of the tree itself. The designers selected an oak leaf with a rounded, not pointed shape: It presented a more friendly personality and allowed them to carve out a smooth moon shape from the tree form itself. They also added a cast shadow, which connected the design to the landscape. In this way, it is both conceptual logo and an actual tree.

"The end results put the major emphasis on the brand's differentiating element, the moon, while still focusing on the tree. It presents a young posture and didn't transmit the idea of a heavily structured company," Chasqueira says. Similarly, the use of carats in place of the letter *A* presented a less corporate posture. "The interruption of the type makes the brand younger by presenting a kind of rupture with predefined positions and concepts."

The new logo for Floresta da Lua (which translates to "Moon Forest") uses negative space to great effect.

LOGO SEARCH

Keywords: **Foods**

Type: ◯ Symbol ◯ Typographic ◯ Combo ⦿ All

1

2

3

4

5

Ⓓ = Design Firm   Ⓒ = Client

1A Ⓓ Karl Design Vienna Ⓒ Wein & Culinaria   1B Ⓓ 01D   1C Ⓓ Bailey Lauerman 2   1D Ⓓ Fandam Studio Ⓒ African Dream Trust

2A Ⓓ Ulyanov Denis Ⓒ Lapsha   2B Ⓓ Judson Design Ⓒ Olympia Grill   2C Ⓓ cruzcontrol design Ⓒ RowMart   2D Ⓓ Tom Law Design Ⓒ Castleberry Hill Events & Catering

3A Ⓓ Squires and Company Ⓒ NOW   3B Ⓓ FUEL Creative Group Ⓒ Kobra Culinary Concepts   3C Ⓓ LAMORA Ⓒ Masterpiece Delicatessen   3D Ⓓ Dezion Studios Ⓒ Baker Printing

4A Ⓓ Youngha Park Ⓒ Noodle York   4B Ⓓ Flywheel Design Ⓒ six plates wine bar   4C Ⓓ Schwartzrock Graphic Arts Ⓒ Target   4D Ⓓ Bailey Lauerman 2

5A Ⓓ Double A Creative Ⓒ Loud Egg Multimedia   5B Ⓓ Doink, Inc. Ⓒ BeachGroceries.com   5C Ⓓ Banowetz + Company, Inc. Ⓒ Breadwinners   5D Ⓓ ESD Ⓒ Cinnamon Toast

	A	B	C	D
1				
2				
3				
4				

Ⓓ = Design Firm   Ⓒ = Client

LOGO SEARCH

Keywords: **Structures**

Type: ○ Symbol ○ Typographic ○ Combo ● All

GEM HOMES

METRO DALLAS HOMELESS ALLIANCE

DJEČJI VRTIĆ KAŠTELA

transcend REALTY

Eco-Products

McCOY REALTY GROUP

CONNIE FULLER REAL ESTATE

OurHouse.com
EVERYTHING YOUR HOUSE DESIRES

ESTD 1984
TRADITIONS HOME

HABITAT FOR HUMANITY RE-STORE

	A	B	C	D
1		 DEVELOPERS RESEARCH	 CENA DI MARE	
2			 BURN CREATIVE	 BROWN'S BREWING Co
3		 MINISTRY STUDIO		 BABEL BOOKSTORE
4	LANGLEY SCHOOL	RIGSBEE HALL	 AUSTURBÆR	 FLORIDA REALTORS
5	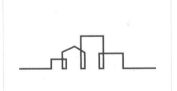	 HANLON	 The Sequoias SAN FRANCISCO	 SKY COUNCIL

A	B	C	D	
		 KOREAN FOOD	 OLDE TOWNE	1
 VELLANO *Tuscan Heart, California Soul.*	 THE MONTEREY			2
	 ТЫСЯЧЕЛЕТИЕ ЯРОСЛАВЛЯ			3
 ASPIRE 夢 JAPAN	EHSAL		 Мельница	4
		 terradisiena		5

Ⓓ = Design Firm Ⓒ = Client

LOGO SEARCH

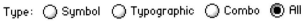

Keywords **Transportation**

Type: ◯ Symbol ◯ Typographic ◯ Combo ⦿ All

iParts.pl

carticipate

Easy

GREEN RAIL

ⅅ = Design Firm   ⓒ = Client

1C ⅅ Karl Design Vienna ⓒ Humanity   1D ⅅ UNIT-Y ⓒ Webster Design Associates

2A ⅅ c3 ⓒ Corporate Id   2B ⅅ Tactix Creative ⓒ US Postal Service   2C ⅅ Velocity Design Group ⓒ Schnepf Farms   2D ⅅ Storm Design Inc. ⓒ Factory 1969

3A ⅅ Pejot ⓒ Hipol   3B ⅅ RARE Design ⓒ FSORBO   3C ⅅ VanPaul Design ⓒ Carticipate   3D ⅅ ezzo Design ⓒ JM Lavagem AutomÃ_vel

4A ⅅ Tower of Babel ⓒ Citizens of the Road   4B ⅅ Cfx ⓒ St. Louis Cellars   4C ⅅ Sayles Graphic Design, Inc. ⓒ Bonneville   4D ⅅ Extra Point Creative ⓒ HALO Racing

5A ⅅ L*U*K*E ⓒ Blue Tractor Cook Shop   5B ⅅ Oscar Morris ⓒ Home Slice Pizzeria   5C ⅅ Bailey Lauerman 2   5D ⅅ Bailey Lauerman 2

1

2

3

4

5

Ⓓ = Design Firm Ⓒ = Client

1A Ⓓ Rocketman Creative Ⓒ Rocketman Creative 1B Ⓓ Vasco Morelli Design Ⓒ Atomic Tango 1C Ⓓ Squires and Company Ⓒ AviEx 1D Ⓓ Greteman Group Ⓒ Kansas Aviation Museum

2A Ⓓ Design Greater Than Ⓒ Front Range Vista 2B Ⓓ INSP 2C Ⓓ Diagram Ⓒ EGAC 2008 2D Ⓓ Diagram Ⓒ Aeroklub Radom

3A Ⓓ Metropolis Advertising Ⓒ Marriott Vacation Club 3B Ⓓ vladimir sijerkovic Ⓒ Two Brothers Canoe 3C Ⓓ Glitschka Studios Ⓒ ReThink Communications 3D Ⓓ Oat Ⓒ S. R. Weiner

4A Ⓓ CF Napa Brand Design Ⓒ Tug Boat, Inc. 4B Ⓓ Thelogoloft.com Ⓒ Caravel 4C Ⓓ Karl Design Vienna Ⓒ Q / Mayflower Capital 4D Ⓓ Karl Design Vienna Ⓒ Q / Mayflower Capital

5A Ⓓ Burocratik—Design 5B Ⓓ ANS Ⓒ Harbour Island Tourist Bureau 5C Ⓓ Greteman Group Ⓒ The Huntington Harbour Philharmonic 5D Ⓓ Roy Smith Design Ⓒ Further

index

Log onto www.logolounge.com/book5 for free electronic access to a database of the logos in this book. Search for logos by keywords, client or design firm name, client industry, or type of mark, and get designer credits and contact information along with the logos. For access to more than 100,000 logos using the same search function, purchase a membership to www.logolounge.com. The collection is always growing: In fact, your membership also allows you to upload an unlimited number of your own logos to be considered by our judges for inclusion in the next LogoLounge book.

directory

Clark Studios, Inc.
United States
949-878-0469
www.clark-studios.com

classic lines design
United Kingdom
01527 882992
www.classiclinesdesign.com

Clay McIntosh Creative
United States
918-591-3070
www.claymcintosh.com

Clusta Ltd
United States
121-604-0044
www.clusta.com

co:lab
United States
860-233-6382
www.colabinc.com

Cody Haltom
United States
405-625-5751
www.codyhaltom.com

cogu design
United States
310-384-1544

The Collaboration
United States
816-474-3232
www.the-collaboration.com

Collaboration Reverberation
United States
858-433-1456
www.collaborationreverberation.com

CONCEPTO WORLDWIDE
Dominican Republic
809 965 6592

concussion, llc
United States
817-336-6824 x 207

Coolstone Design Works, Inc.
United States
206-204-5678
www.coolstone.com

Corder Philips
United States
704-333-3924
www.corderphilips.com

Counterpart Communication Design
United States
901-323-4900
www.counterpartcd.com

Cre@ive Design Advertising
New Zealand
064 6 872 8400
www.thecreativeshow.co.nz

Creative Beard
United States
949-413-3774
www.creativebeard.com

Creative Conspiracy Inc.
United States
970-247-2262

Creative Madhouse
United States
817-903-2583
www.creativemadhouse.com

Creative NRG
United States
414-305-1578
www.creative-nrg.com

Cricket Design Works
United States
608-255-0002
www.cricketdesignworks.com

Crosby Associates
United States
312-346-2900
www.crosbyassociates.com

CrossGrain Creative Studios
United States
714-628-9586
www.crossgrain.com

cruzcontrol design
United States
312-401-9969
www.cruzcontroldesign.com

Cubic
United States
918-587-7888
www.cubiccreative.com

Curtis Sharp Design
United States
206-366-7975
www.curtissharpdesign.com

cypher13
United States
720-562-0193
www.cypher13.com

D&Dre Creative
United States
512-577-9189
www.ape-texas.com/deandrecreative

D&i (Design and Image)
United States
303-292-3455
www.seebrandgo.com

dache
Switzerland
+41 78 683 37 59
www.dache.ch

DAGSVERK—Design and Advertising
Iceland
354-588-1350
www.dagsverk.is

dale harris
Australia
411899840
www.daleharris.com

Daniel Matthews
United Kingdom
+44(0)7734592041
www.danielmatthews.net

Dara Creative
Ireland
00 353 1 672 5222
www.daracreative.ie

Darkstone&Cardinal
Poland
+ 48 042 632 17 51
www.darkstone-cardinal.pl

David Beck Design
United States
214-828-9622

David Gramblin
United States
918-261-2042

David Maloney
United States
612-396-2548
www.david-maloney.com

Davis Design
United States
303-399-8111
www.davisdesign.net

DBD+A Studio
United States
503-679-1701

DDB SF
United States
415-732-2235
www.ddbsf.com

debut
United Kingdom
1902837424
www.debutcreate.com

Deep Design
United States
404-266-7500
www.deepdesign.com

Delineate
United States
240-793-5613
www.delineatedesign.com

demasijones
Australia
+618 8212 9065
www.demasijones.com

Denis Olenik Design Studio
Belarus
+37529 7580457
www.denisolenik.com

Dennard, Lacey & Associates
United States
972-233-0430
www.dennardlacey.com

The Department of Marketing
United States
919-256-3793
www.thedofm.com

Design Army
United States
202-797-1018
www.designarmy.com

Design Farm
United States
310-266-5921
www.designfarmstudios.com

Design Forum
United States
937-439-4400
www.designforum.com

Design Greater Than
United States
970-214-3024
www.designgreaterthan.com

Design Hovie Studios, Inc.
United States
206-783-8600
www.hovie.com

Designer Case
Poland
502221797
www.designercase.net

designheavy
United States
206-781-3477
www.designheavy.com

DesignPoint, Inc.
United States
503-364-2970
www.designpointinc.com

Designwerke Inc.
Canada
416-362-6000
www.designwerke.com

DesignWorks Group
United States
940-696-1229
www.designworksgroup.com

Dessein
Australia
61.8.9228.0661
www.dessein.com.au

DEVELOPED IMAGE PTE LTD
Singapore
65 97862302

Dezion Studios
United States
918-557-3695
www.dezion.com

diadik
United States
918-269-3151

Diagram
Poland
48618862079
www.diagram.pl

Digital Flannel
United States
802-457-3838
www.digitalflannel.com

Digital Slant
United States
435-755-5783
www.digitalslant.com

DikranianDesign
United States
813-247-5223
www.dikraniandesign.com

Dill and Company
United States
301-760-7282
www.dillandcompany.org

Doink, Inc.
United States
305-529-0121
www.doinkdesign.com

Dotzero Design
United States
503-892-9262
www.dotzerodesign.com

Double A Creative
United States
402-719-5362
www.doubleacreative.com

Double Brand
Poland
+48 61 6625400
www.doublebrand.pl

Dragulescu Studio
United States
323-919-1521
www.dragulescu.com

The Drawing Board
United States
352-346-8948
www.tdbgraphics.com

Dreambox Creative
United States
916-705-0406
www.dreamboxcreative.com

Driving Force
United Arab Emirates
www.d4rce.com

Duffy & Partners
United States
612-548-2333
www.duffy.com

DUSTIN PARKER ARTS
United States
316-993-1397
www.dustinparkerarts.com

E. Tage Larsen Design
United States
917-881-2863
www.etagelarsen.com

e-alw.com
Poland
48 602229544
www.e-alw.com

East 14th Creative, Inc.
United States
336-288-0939
www.e14c.com

Eben Design
United States
206-523-9010
www.ebendesign.com

Effusion Creative Solutions
United States
480-227-8951
www.effusiondesign.com

Eggra
Macedonia, The Former Yugoslav
Republic Of
38970390144
www.eggra.com

EHA
Denmark
45 40955180
www.eha.dk

eight a.m. brand design
(shanghai) Co., Ltd
China
8621 61313958
www.8-a-m.com

El Creative
United States
214-742-0700
www.elcreative.com

El Paso, Galeria de Comunicacion
Spain
+34 91 594 22 48
www.elpasocomunicacion.com

elbow
United States
415-738-8833
www.elbow.com

eldesign.ru
Russia
79262207316

Eli Atkins Design
United States
831-420-4053

Eli Kirk
United States
801-377-9321
www.elikirk.com

ellen bruss design
United States
303-830-8323
www.ebd.com

Emblem
United States
512-771-3593
www.emblemcreative.com

Entermotion Design Studio
United States
316-264-2277
www.entermotion.com

Entropy Brands
United States
406-599-3490
www.entropybrands.com

Envision Creative Group
United States
512-292-1049
www.envision-creative.com

The Eppstein Group
United States
817-737-3656
www.eppsteingroup.com

Erwin-Penland, Inc.
United States
864-672-5583
www.erwinpenland.com

ESD
South Africa
117040943

Essex Two
United States
773-489-1400
www.sx2.com

eurie creative
United States
702-383-9805
www.euriecreative.com

ex nihilo
Belgium
0032 65 62 25 58
www.exnihilo.be

Exhibit A: Design Group
Canada
604-873-1583
www.exhibitadesigngroup.com

EXPLORARE
Mexico
52 (222) 230-4152
www.explorare.com

Extra Point Creative
United States
407-312-2427
www.extrapointcreative.com

eye4 inc.
United States
352-338-7519
www.eye4.com

ezzo Design
Portugal
+351 229969263

face
United Kingdom
01423 561780
www.face-group.co.uk

Factor Tres
Mexico
525555567178
www.factortres.com.mx

Fandam Studio
South Africa
+27(0)829017699

Felixsockwell.com
United States
917-657-8880
www.felixsockwell.com

Fernandez Design
United States
512-619-4020
www.fernandezdesign.com

Fifth Letter
United States
336-723-5655
www.fifth-letter.com

Filthy Clothing
United Kingdom
+44 (0)7712 834 711
www.filthy.co.nz

Finch Creative
United States
713-490-1000
www.finchcreative.com

Firehouse
United States
972-692-0918
www.fhdallas.com

FIRON
Russia
+7 495 798 6990
www.firon.com

Fischer Design
United States
310-314-2246
www.hankfischer.com

Fiton
Iceland
+354 8220776
www.fiton.is

FiveNineteen: a print + motion + interactive design boutique.
United States
918-948-5190
www.fivenineteen.com

Fixation Marketing
United States
240-207-2009
www.fixation.com

Fleishman Hillard
United States
314-982-7701

The Flores Shop
United States
804-496-6616
www.thefloresshop.com

Flow Creative
United States
773-276-4425
www.flowcreative.net

Fluid Studio
United States
801-295-9820
www.fluid-studio.net

Flywheel Design
United States
919-683-8164
www.flywheeldesign.com

For the Love of Creating
United States
770-516-7301
www.fortheloveofcreating.com

ForeScene & Your Eyes Here
United States
410-420-2491
www.foresceneweb.com

Forthright Strategic Design
United States
415-205-4466
www.forthrightdesign.com

Franke+Fiorella
United States
612-338-1700
www.frankefiorella.com

Freeman Design
United States
907-258-0603

Fresh Design
Ireland
01 672 9440
www.fresh.ie

Fresh Oil
United States
401-709-4656
www.freshoil.com

Freshwater Design
United States
678-910-6381
www.rhondafreshwater.com

FUEL Creative Group
United States
916-669-1591

Fuelhaus Brand Strategy + Design
United States
619-574-1342
www.fuelhaus.com

fuszion
United States
703-548-8080
www.fuszion.com

futska llc
United States
719-235-8451
www.futska.com

FutureBrand
Australia
+61 3 9604 2777
www.futurebrand.com

FutureBrand BC&H
Brazil
55 11 38211166
www.futurebrand.com

Fuze
United States
775-626-4577
www.ifuze.com

Galperin Design, Inc.
United States
212-873-1121
www.galperindesign.com

Gardner Design
United States
316-691-8808
www.gardnerdesign.com

Gary Sample Design
United States
513-271-7785

GCG Advertising
United States
817-332-4600
www.gcgadvertising.com

GDNSS
United States
212-866-1449
www.gdnss.com

Gee + Chung Design
United States
415-543-1192
www.geechungdesign.com

Gesture Studio
United States
713-808-9342
www.gesturestudio.com

Gibson
United Kingdom
020 8948 9656
www.thisisgibson.com

Giles Design Inc.
United States
210-224-8378
www.gilesdesign.com

GingerBee Creative
United States
406-443-3032
www.gingerbeecreative.net

Gingerbread Lady
United Kingdom
447887811070
www.gingerbread-lady.co.uk

Ginter & Miletina
Germany
+49 611-7243803
www.ginter-miletina.de

Giorgio Davanzo Design
United States
206-328-5031
www.davanzodesign.com

Gizwiz Studio
Malaysia
604 228 9931
www.logodesigncreation.com

Glitschka Studios
United States
971-223-6143
www.glitschka.com

The Globe Advertising + Design
Australia
+618 9470 3454
www.the-globe.com.au

Go Media
United States
216-939-0000
www.gomedia.us

Go Welsh
United States
717-898-9000
www.gowelsh.com

Goloubinov
Russia
+7(909)635-93-25

Graphic design studio
by Yurko Gutsulyak
Ukraine
380674465560
www.gstudio.com.ua

Graphic Nincompoop
Iceland
+354 697 9012
www.graphicnincompoop.com

Graphics & Designing Inc.
Japan
+81-3-3449-0651
www.gandd.co.jp

Graphismo
United States
512-686-1495
www.graphismo.com

Green Olive Media
United States
404-815-9327
www.greenolivemedia.com

Greteman Group
United States
316-263-1004
www.gretemangroup.com

GSW Worldwide
United States
614-543-6753

guten tag!
United States
920-426-8078
www.gutentag.us

Gyula Németh
Hungary
36 20 429 2019
www.seadevilworks.blogspot.com

H2 Design of Texas
United States
512-775-7350
www.h2dot.com

HA Design
United States
626-475-6606

Habitat Design
United States
404-784-1276
www.designbyhabitat.com

Haley Johnson Design Co.
United States
612-722-8050
www.hjd.com

Hand dizajn studio
Croatia
38512333489
www.hand.hr

Haven Productions
United States
615-794-0354
www.havenproductions.net

Hayes Image
Australia
52484816

Hayes+Company
Canada
416-536-5438
www.hayesandcompany.com

Hazen Creative, Inc.
United States
312-451-5413
www.hazencreative.com

Headshot brand development
Ukraine
380442781031
www.headshot.tm.ua

Headspring Design
Canada
9056277979
www.headspring.ca

Heather Boyce-Broddle
United States
316-744-6267

Hecht Design
United States
781-643-1988
www.hechtdesign.com

Heisel Design
United States
941-922-0492
www.heiseldesign.com

Helena Seo Design
United States
408-830-0086
www.helenaseo.com

Helius Creative Advertising
United States
801-673-4199
www.freewebs.com/utahrugbyguy

Hemmo.nl
The Netherlands
31620272777
www.hemmo.nl

HendrixRaderWise
United States
317-251-4332

Hero Design Studio
United States
303-832-3310
www.herodesignstudio.com

Herrainco Brand Strategy + Design
Canada
604-688-5334

Hexanine
United States
773-678-9951
www.hexanine.com

Hiebing
United States
608-256-6357
www.hiebing.com

High Tide Creative
United States
252-671-7087
www.hightidecreative.com

Hill Design Studios
United States
503-507-1228
www.hilldesignstudios.com

Hirschmann Design
United States
303-449-7363

Hoet & Hoet
Belgium
+ 32 2 646 40 06
www.hoet-hoet.eu

Home Grown Logos
United States
707-338-1271
www.homegrownlogos.com

Honey Design
Canada
519-679-0786
www.honey.on.ca

HOOK
United States
843-853-5532
www.hookusa.com

Hornall Anderson
United States
206-467-5800
www.hadw.com

Hotwire, Inc
United States
508-386-3841
www.hotwireindustries.com

Howerton+White
United States
316-262-6644
www.howertonwhite.com

Hubbell Design Works
United States
714-227-3457
www.hubbelldesignworks.com

Hula+Hula
Mexico
52 55 56 84 73 62
www.hulahula.com.mx

Hutner Group
United States
415-309-1868
www.hutnergroup.com

Hvita husid
Iceland
+354 562 1177

ICG
United Kingdom
01772 679 383
www.icgonline.co.uk

id29
United States
518-687-0268
www.id29.com

IdeaWorks—Brand ID
Australia
61299094440
www.ideaworks.com.au

Identica Branding and Design
Canada
604-647-6223
www.identica.com

IF marketing & advertising
United States
512-930-5558
www.yourifteam.com

Ikola Designs
United States
763-533-3440

Illustra Graphics
United States
717-679-2390
www.illustra-graphics.com

Imadesign, Corp.
Russia
+7 495-729-5693
www.imadesign.ru

Image Public, Inc.
United States
917-573-4038
www.imagepublic.com

Imaginaria
United States
972-423-1232
www.imaginariacreative.com

INDE
Greece
(0030) 6937239568
www.behance.net/inde_graphics

Indigo Creative
United States
805-450-6844
www.indigocreativestudio.com

Inertia Graphics
United States
301-714-2282
www.designsbyig.com

INSP
United States
803-578-1236
www.robcheney.com

Integrated Communications (ICLA)
United States
310-851-8066
www.icla.com

Integrated Media, Inc.
United States
317-508-5022

Interbrand São Paulo
Brazil
+55 11 3707-8500
www.interbrand.com

Iperdesign, Inc.
United States
917-412-9045
www.iperdesign.com

ism
United States
617-353-1822
www.ismboston.com

Ivan Manolov
Bulgaria
+359 889 277 395
www.behance.net/adder

Ivey McCoig Creative Partners
United States
615-472-8238
www.iveymccoig.com

Jajo, Inc.
United States
316-267-6700
www.jajo.net

James Arthur & Company
United States
618-997-6298
www.jamesarthurco.com

James Kelly
United Kingdom
www.firemusic.co.uk

Jan Sabach Design
Czech Republic
420733264557
www.sabach.cz

Jank Design
United States
917-701-5133
www.jankdesign.com

Jarek Kowalczyk
Poland
+48 502634695
www.jarekkowalczyk.com

Javen Design
United States
718-347-2704
www.javendesign.com

Jeff Andrews Design
United States
503-269-2944
www.jeffandrewsdesign.com

Jeffhalmos
Canada
416-850-9616
www.jeffhalmos.com

Jeni Olsen Design
United States
707-479-1734
www.jeniolsendesign.com

jenn gula design
United States
216-832-2679
www.jennguladesign.com

Jennifer Braham Design
United States
512-707-9023

Jerron Ames
United States
801-770-2904

Jerry Kuyper Partners
United States
203-451-4023
www.jerrykuyper.com

JG Creative
United States
208-440-2301

Jill Bell Brandlettering
United States
913-649-4505
www.jillbell.com

Jill Carson
United States
336-723-7572

jing
United States
216-272-7398

JINIZM
United States
831-905-1557
www.jinizm.com

jKaczmarek
United States
www.jkaczmarek.com

Jobi
United Arab Emirates
971504943676

The Joe Bosack Graphic Design Co.
United States
215-766-1461
www.joebosack.com

Joel Storey Design
United States
919-815-1323
www.joelstorey.com

Jon Duarte Design Group
United States
808-550-8179
www.jonduarte.com

Jon Flaming Design
United States
972-235-4880
www.jonflaming.com

Jon Kay Design
United States
352-870-8438
www.jonkaydesign.com

joni dunbar design
United States
601-520-3309

Josef Stapel
Germany
496190931907
www.josefstapel.de

josh higgins design
United States
619-379-2090
www.joshhiggins.com

JoshuaCreative
United States
559-906-0504

Jovan Rocanov
Serbia
381112972006
www.rocanov.com

joven orozco design
United States
949-723-1898
www.jovenville.com

juancazu
Argentina
1567847542

Judson Design
United States
713-520-1096
www.judsondesign.com

Juice Media
United States
702-433-4086
www.juicemultimedia.com

julian peck
United States
415-246-4897

Just Creative Design
Australia
+61 411 402 312
www.justcreativedesign.com

K2 Creative, Inc.
United States
630-460-7091
www.k2chicago.com

Kahn Design
United States
760-944-5574
www.kahn-design.com

Karl Design Vienna
Austria
0043-1-208 66 53
www.karl-design-logos.com

Kastelov
Bulgaria
359886034151
www.kastelov.com

Kate Resnick
United States
202-487-1414

Kessler Digital Design
United States
215-500-3204
www.kesslerdigital.com

Kevin France Design, Inc.
United States
336-765-6213

The Key
Australia
+381 64 3956 793
www.whproject.com

Kille Design
Australia
61413412111
www.kille.com.au

King Design Office
United States
626-304-0848
www.kingdesignoffice.com

Kirk Miller
United States
773-316-9497
www.kirkmiller.us

KITA™ | Visual Playground
Germany
+49.30.54714690
www.kita-berlin.com

Kloom
Brazil
+55 (11) 3337-2607

KNOWGOODER
United States
303-618-6309
www.knowgooder.com

Kobalto
Spain
+34 629442115
www.kobalto.com

Koch Creative Group
United States
316-828-2208
www.kochcreativegroup.com

Koetter Design
United States
502-515-3092

Kolar Advertising and Marketing
United States
512-345-6658
www.kolaradvertising.com

Kommunikat
Poland
602820318
www.kommunikat.pl

Kommunikation & Design
Germany
497751897400
www.kommunikation-design.de

Koray Sahan
Turkey
902122902810

KROG, d.o.o.
Slovenia
+386 41 780 880
www.krog.si

KTD
United States
512-789-6473
www.designluminosity.com

Kurt Snider Design
United States
702-767-1536

Kuznets
Russia
79101517929
www.kuznets.net

L*U*K*E
United States
612-342-9701

La Visual
United States
805-582-2140
www.lavisual.com

Label Kings
United States
2127191245
www.labelkings.com

LaMonica Design
United States
913-593-9644
www.lamonicadesign.com

LAMORA
United States
303-217-3976
www.jorgelamora.com

Landor Associates
Australia
+61 2 8908 8711
www.landor.com

The Laster Group
United States
915-581-7900
www.lastergroup.com

Launchpad Creative
United States
405-514-5158
www.launchpad321.com

legofish
Canada
416-975-0084
www.legofish.com

LEKKERWERKEN
Germany
+49 (611) 34109932
www.lekkerwerken.com

LeoDesign
Indonesia
622139830118
www.leodesignjakarta.com

Level B Design
United States
515-669-8418
www.levelbdesign.com

Levy Innovations
United States
312-932-4937

LGA / Jon Cain
United States
980-253-3336
www.joncain.com

Lienhart Design
United States
312-738-2200
www.lienhartdesign.com

Liew Design, Inc.
United States
650-962-8103
www.liewdesign.com

Lightship Visual
Australia
61894477363
www.lightshipvisual.com

Lilagan Pandji Design
Australia
+61 3 9419 61 64

LIOBmedia
United States
202-625-4334
www.liobmedia.com

Lippincott
United States
212-521-0000
www.lippincott.com

Liquid Agency
United States
408-850-8833
www.liquidagency.com

Liquid Comma
Australia
61418817305

Mattson Creative
United States
949-651-8740
www.mattsoncreative.com

Liquid Inc.
United States
303-282-8657
www.givingideasshape.com

Liquid Pixel Studio
United States
917-319-0413
liquidpixelstudio.net

Little Jacket
United States
720-227-0519
www.little-jacket.com

Lizette Gecel
United States
804-359-1711

logobyte
Turkey
905356666292
www.logobyte.com

LogoDesignGuru.com
United States
877-525-5646
www.logodesignguru.com

Logoholik
Serbia
914 595 6926
www.logoholik.com

Logoidentity.com
United States
908-665-6878
www.logoidentity.com

Loop Design
United States
718-797-2465
www.loopdesigngroup.com

Luke Despatie & The Design Firm
Canada
416-995-0243
www.thedesignfirm.ca

lunabrand design group
United States
480-429-3774
www.lunabrands.com

Lunchbox Design Studio
United States
305-790-1885

Lynde Design
United States
212-203-1554
www.lynde.net

M. Brady Clark Design
United States
512-698-9025
www.mbradyclark.com

m|sane industries
United States
617-577-6468
www.msaneindustries.com

M3 Advertising Design
United States
702-876-3316
www.m3ad.com

MacLaren McCann Calgary
Canada
403-261-7155

Macnab Design
United States
505-286-8558
www.macnabdesign.com

Madomat
United Kingdom
442072297070

Manifest Communications
Canada
416-593-7017
www.manifestcom.com

Marblehead
United States
972-588-3317
www.marbleheadllc.com

markatos | moore
United States
415-235-9203
www.mm-sf.com

Marlin
United States
417-885-4530
www.marlinco.com

Martin Branding Worldwide
United States
804-282-3100
www.martinbranding.com

The Martin Group
United States
716-853-2757
www.martingroupmarketing.com

Martin Jordan
Germany
+49-177-5035307
www.martinjordan.de

Matchstic
United States
404-446-1511
www.matchstic.com

Matt Barratt Design
Australia
61418817305

Mattson Creative
United States
949-651-8740
www.mattsoncreative.com

Mauck Groves Branding & Design
United States
515-288-5278
www.mauckgroves.com

Maycreate
United States
423-634-0123
www.maycreate.com

McConnell Creative
United States
248-420-9148

McDill Design
United States
414-277-8111
www.mcdilldesign.com

McGarrah/Jessee
United States
512-225-2000
www.mc-j.com

McGuire Design
United States
210-884-4609
www.mcguiredesign.com

the medium
United States
425-888-1696
www.the-medium.net

Megan Thompson Design
United States
609-439-1323
www.mtdstudio.com

Meir Billet Ltd.
Israel
+972-3-5627577

MendeDesign
United States
415-431-8200
www.mendedesign.com

metaforma design
Italy
+39 02 45491421
www.metaformadesign.com

Metropolis Advertising
United States
407-835-8080
www.metropolisadvertising.com

Mez Design
United States
415-331-4523
www.mezdesign.com

Michael Freimuth Creative
United States
773-396-1620
www.michaelfreimuth.com

Michael O'Connell
United States
904-705-4437

Michael Patrick Partners
United States
503-796-7777
www.michaelpatrickpartners.com

Mikhail Gubergrits
Russia
+7 985 774 24 08
www.linii.ru

milano.design
United States
561-422-9906
www.milanodesigninc.com

Miles Design
United States
317-915-8693
www.milesdesign.com

Milk Creative Services
Ukraine
+380 50 4621869
www.milk.ua

Miller Creative LLC
United States
732-600-3933
www.yaelmiller.com

millspaz design
United States
785-312-9101
www.millspaz.com

Mindgruve
United States
619-757-1325
www.mindgruve.com

Mindpower Inc.
United States
404-581-1991
www.mindpowerinc.com

Mindspike Design
United States
414-765-2344
www.mindspikedesign.com

MINE™
United States
415-647-6463
www.minesf.com

mIQelangelo
Serbia
381641179800
www.miqelangelo.com

Miriello Grafico, Inc.
United States
866-647-4355
www.miriellografico.com

Mirko Ilic Corp
United States
212-481-9737
www.mirkoilic.com

Mitre Agency
United States
336-230-0575
www.mitreagency.com

The Mixx
United States
212-695-6663
www.themixxnyc.com

mod&co
United States
612-238-3930
www.modandco.com

Mojo Solo
United States
651-789-6656
www.mojosolo.com

Moker Ontwerp
The Netherlands
+31(0)20 3307720
www.mokerontwerp.nl

monkeebox inc.
United States
703-606-9044
www.monkeebox.com

Monster Design Company
United States
707-208-5481
www.monsterdesignco.com

moosylvania
United States
314-644-7900
www.moosylvania.com

MSDS
United States
212-925-6460
www.ms-ds.com

MSI
United States
312-946-6146
www.msinet.com

Muamer Adilovic DESIGN
Bosnia & Herzegovina
+387 61 202 597
www.logotip.ba

MUELLER design
United States
510-763-8583
www.muellerdesign.com

mugur mihai
Romania
+40 723 652336
www.mugurmihai.com

Muku Studios
United States
808-225-6858
www.mukustudios.com

MultiAdaptor
United Kingdom
+44 (0)20 7613 1103
www.multiadaptor.com

Murillo Design, Inc.
United States
210-248-9412
www.murillodesign.com

My Card, My work.
United States
617-792-3378
www.mycardmywork.com

Natale Design
United States
480-241-8811
www.nataledesign.com

Nectar Graphics
United States
503-472-1512
www.nectargraphics.com

NeoGrafica
Costa Rica
506-4400061
www.neografica.net

Newhouse Design
United States
406-600-6532
www.newhousedesign.com

Neworld Associates
Ireland
35314165600
www.neworld.ie

nGen Works
United States
904-399-4411
www.ngenworks.com

Nicole Romer
Australia
61425806177
www.nicoleromer.com.au

Nicole Ziegler
United States
717-372-0437
www.nicolezieglerdesign.com

Nissen Design
United States
503-363-5639

nixture
United States
504-251-7602
www.nicollek.com

noe design
United States
515-597-4286
www.noedesign.com

northfound
United States
215-232-6420
www.northfound.com

NOT A CANNED HAM
United States
404-316-2132

NOVOGRAMA
Mexico
(52)(477) 1437163
www.novograma.com

Nynas
United States
214-566-5166

o.pudov
Russia
+7 903 6822604

Oat
United States
617-800-2636
www.oatcreative.com

Obnocktious
United States
469-450-4325
www.obnocktious.com

Octavo Designs
United States
301-695-8885
www.8vodesigns.com

ODA
United States
415-970-8400

ODM oficina de diseño y marketing
Spain
34956265326
www.odmoficina.com

Offbeat Design
United States
734-214-1996
www.offbeatdesign.com

The Office of Art+Logik
United States
612-599-0286

Officina delle idee
Italy
390309959380
www.officinadelleidee.net

ohTwentyone
United States
817-504-7550
www.ohtwentyone.com

Oliver Russell
United States
208-344-1734
www.oliverrussell.com

Oluzen
Dominican Republic
809 852 9907
www.oluzen.com

O'Mahony Design LLC
United States
941-377-8168
www.omahonydesign.com

One Minute Hero
Poland
48506758581
www.oneminutehero.com

ONEDRINPEN
United Kingdom
www.onedrinpen.com

Oomingmak Design Company
United States
817-983-0142

Open Creative Group
United States
205-437-3395
www.opencreativegroup.com

Opolis Design, LLC
United States
503-287-7722
www.opolisdesign.com

ORFIK DESIGN
Greece
306932909191
www.orfikdesign.gr

Origami
Canada
877.674.4264
www.origami.qc.ca

orton design
United States
801-691-8244

Oscar Morris
United States
512-293-5954

Ostrov Svobody
Russia
74955046341
www.os-design.ru

Oxide Design Co.
United States
402-344-0168
www.oxidedesign.com

Ozidea
Ukraine
+38 044 331 98 86

p11creative
United States
714-641-2090
www.p11.com

Pale Horse Design
United States
727-823-6202
www.palehorsedesign.com

Palmerlee Design
United States
347-248-6967
www.palmerleedesign.com

Pandemonium Creative
Australia
03 9690 1511

PaperSky Design
United States
408-340-7902
www.paperskydesign.com

Pappas Group
United States
703-349-7221
www.pappasgroup.com

Parachute Design
United States
612-339-3902
www.parachutedesign.com

Paradigm New Media Group
United States
314-621-7600
www.pnmg.com

Paradox Box
Russia
79177519251
www.paradoxbox.ru

Parallel Creative Group
United States
423-228-2971
www.parallelcreativegroup.com

paralleldesigned
United States
415-867-9149
www.paralleldesigned.com

Park Avenue Design
United States
732-363-7297
www.parkavegraphics.com

Parker White
United States
760-783-2020
www.parkerwhite.com

Passing Notes, Inc.
United States
510-835-8035
www.passing-notes.com

Patten ID
United States
517-627-2033

Paul Jobson
United States
864-420-8998
www.pauljobson.com

Paul Svancara
United States
480-580-5667
www.svancdesign.com

Pavone
United States
717-234-8886
www.pavone.net

Pawel Tomas "Substrate"
Poland
www.substrate.pl

Peak Seven
United States
954-574-0810
www.peakseven.com

pearpod
United States
949-361-8900
www.pearpod.com

Pearson Education Ltd
United Kingdom
01865 311366

Pejot
Poland
+48 601377156
www.pejot.com

Penhouse Design
Ireland
353 57 862 5522
www.penhouse.ie

Periscope
United States
612-399-0500
www.periscope.com

Peterson Ray & Company
United States
214-215-7360

Phil Foss Design
United States
703-850-6259

Phinney/Bischoff Design House
United States
206-322-3484
www.pbdh.com

Phixative
United States
212-534-9058

Phony Lawn
United States
720-273-1414
www.phonylawn.com

Piccirilli Group, Inc.
United States
410-879-6780
www.picgroup.com

pictogram studio
United States
301-962-9630

Pierpoint Design + Branding
United States
509-466-1565
www.pierpointwebsite.com

Pikant marketing
Croatia
38548222127

The Pink Pear Design Company
United States
816-519-7327
www.pinkpear.com

Pink Tank Creative
Australia
61294841239
www.pinktank.com.au

Plumbline Studios
United States
707-251-9884
www.plumbline.com

POLLARDdesign
United States
503-246-7251
www.pollarddesign.com

Popgun
United States
415-503-0108
www.popgun.com

Porkka & Kuutsa Oy
Finland
+358 207401696
www.porkka-kuutsa.fi

Prana Design + Art Studios
Australia
+61 413007899
www.pranastudios.com.au

Prejean Creative
United States
337-593-9051
www.prejeancreative.com

PULK
Germany
0049 30 31 98 40 158
www.pulk-berlin.com

Pumpkinfish
United States
954-563-5690
www.pumpkinfish.com

Pure Identity Design
United States
262-653-8000
www.pureidentitydesign.com

Quantum Communications/
Brandcentral
Lebanon
9611204613
www.brandcentral.cc

Quentin Duncan
South Africa
+27 84 553 1616

R Design LLC
United States
720-933-3816
www.rdesignllc.com

R&R Partners
United States
702-228-0222
www.rrpartners.com

Rain Design
Australia
613 9826 5707

Raise Studio
United States
404-373-3460
www.raisestudio.com

Ramp
United States
213-623-7267
www.rampcreative.com

Range
United States
214-744-0555
www.rangeus.com

RARE Design
United States
601-544-7273
www.raredesign.com

Ray Dugas Design
United States
334-844-3384
www.cadc.auburn.edu/graphicdesign/ray.html

raykodesign
Germany
00492183-416338
www.raykodesign.de

Razor Creative
Canada
(506) 382-4200
www.razorcreative.com

RDQLUS Creative
United States
402-212-0108
www.rdqlus.com

Re Generate Design
Canada
416-703-1983

Reaction Design & Printing
United States
760-327-3641
www.reactiondp.com

Reactive Mediums
United States
517-290-6156

reaves design
United States
773-552-2040
www.wbreaves.com

Red Olive Design
United States
801-545-0410
www.redolivedesign.com

RedBrand
Russia
+7(495) 772-39-39
www.golovach.ru/works

redkai
United Kingdom
+44 (0)845 257 5722
www.redkai.com

Redspine Design
United States
972-731-9539

Relevant Studio
United States
505-553-9359
www.relevantstudio.com

resonate design
Ireland
35318535261
www.resonate.ie

Respiro Media
Romania
40724551837
www.relogodesign.com

Reveal Creative
United States
425-827-1283
www.revealcreative.com

Rhombus, Inc.
United States
206-441-1061
www.rhombusdesign.net

Richard Ward Associates
United Kingdom
020 8542 7536

Richards Brock Miller Mitchell &
Associates
United States
214-987-6500
www.rbmm.com

Rickabaugh Graphics
United States
614-337-2229
www.rickabaughgraphics.com

RIGGS
United States
803-799-5972
www.riggspeak.com

The Right Hand
United States
646-250-9405

Riley Designs
United States
970-927-9261
www.rileyhutchens.com

RIZN Communication Design
Bulgaria
+359 886 815 349
www.kaloiantoshev.com

Rob McClurkan Illustration
United States
770-597-7374
www.seerobdraw.com

robin ott design
United States
330-465-6261
www.robinottdesign.com

The Robin Shepherd Group
United States
904-359-0981
www.trsg.net

RocketDog Communications
United States
206-254-0248
www.rocketdog.org

Rocketlab Creative
United States
512-431-5426

Rocketman Creative
United States
858-663-5082
www.rocketmancreative.com

Roman Kotikov
Russia
+7 920 025 05 20

Rome & Gold Creative
United States
505-897-0870
www.rgcreative.com

Rosendahl Grafikdesign
Germany
00 49 30 44 01 28 00
www.rosendahlgrafik.de

Roskelly Inc.
United States
401-683-5091
www.roskelly.com

The Royal We
United States
316-258-2036
www.theroyalweisus.com

Roy Smith Design
United Kingdom
+44 (0)7767 797525
www.roysmithdesign.com

Rubber Design
United States
415-626-2990
www.rubberdesign.com

Rubin Cordaro Design
United States
612-343-0011
www.rubincordaro.com

Rumfang
Denmark
4533692070
www.rumfang.dk

The Russo Group
United States
337-962-4612
www.therussogroup.com

RWest
United States
503-223-5443
www.rwestideas.com

Ryan Ford Design
United States
714-642-4696
www.liquisoft.com

Ryan Kegley
United States
816-728-5049
www.ryankegley.com

Ryan Smoker Design
United States
717-394-6932
www.ryansmoker.com

rylander design
United States
415-389-1998
www.rylanderdesign.com

S Design, Inc.
United States
405-608-0556
www.sdesigninc.com

S4LE.com
Canada
905-467-7139
www.s4le.com

Sabingrafik, Inc.
United States
760-431-0439
www.tracy.sabin.com

Sagetopia
United States
703-726-6400
www.sagetopia.com

Sakkal Design
United States
425-483-8830
www.sakkal.com

Sally Says
United States
773-633-3124
www.sallysays.com

Sampartners
Korea
82-2-508-7871
www.sampartners.co.kr

San Markos
Poland
022 321 51 00
www.sanmarkos.pl

Sandstrom Design
United States
503-248-9466
www.sandstromdesign.com

Sayles Graphic Design, Inc.
United States
515-279-2922
www.saylesdesign.com

Schwartzrock Graphic Arts
United States
952-994-7625
www.schwartzrock.com

SCORR Marketing
United States
308-237-5567
www.scorrmarketing.com

Seamer Design
Australia
03 94157727
www.seamerdesign.com

Sebastiany Branding & Design
Brazil
55 11 3926-3937
www.sebastiany.com.br

Severance Digital Studio
United States
559-271-1158

Shawn Huff
United States
850-968-5736
www.shawnhuff.info

Shift Thinkers
Portugal
351214135760
www.shiftthinkers.com

Shotgun Front Ltd
United Kingdom
01590 677664

Sibley Peteet
United States
512-473-2333
www.spdaustin.com

Sinclair & Co.
United States
919-833-9102
www.sinclair-co.com

Skin Designstudio
Norway
+47 922 97 019
www.skin.no

Skybend
United States
801-983-6760
www.skybend.com

Small Dog Design
Australia
61 3 5333 7777
www.smalldog.com.au

Smith Design
United States
973-429-2177
www.smithdesign.com

Snap Creative
United States
314-482-6438

SO2 DESIGN
Switzerland
+4122 781 5060
www.so2design.ch

Sockeye Creative
United States
503-226-3843
www.sockeyecreative.com

Sol Consultores
Mexico
(011)(525)56586300
www.solconsultores.com.mx

Sommese Design
United States
814-353-1951

Soren Severin
Denmark
(+45) 5126 2482
www.sorenseverin.dk

SOUL
United States
631-240-9153
www.soulnyc.com

Sour Cream Glaze
United States
716-517-6298

SourceMecca
United States
626-644-0710
www.sourcemecca.com

soViet
Australia
+61 (0) 419 394 575
www.soviet.com.au

Spark Studio
Australia
+613 9686 4703
www.sparkstudio.com.au

Special Modern Design
United States
323-258-1212
www.specialmoderndesign.com

Spela Draslar
Slovenia
00 386 31 879 711

Splash:Design
Canada
250-868-1059
www.splashdesign.biz

Spoonbend
United States
512-473-2500
www.spoonbend.com

Spork Design, Inc.
United States
614-228-0900
www.sporkdesign.com

Spring Advertising + Design
Canada
604-683-0167
www.springadvertising.com

squiggle6
Australia
+612 9337 2532
www.squiggle6.com

Squires and Company
United States
214-939-9194
www.squirescompany.com

Steve Cantrell
United States
954-574-0601

Steve Dunphy & Co.
United States
917-744-9046

Steve's Portfolio
United States
215-840-0880
www.stevesportfolio.net

Stiles Design
United States
512-633-9247
www.brettstilesdesign.com

Storm Design Inc.
Canada
403-239-9401
www.stormdesigninc.com

Strategic America
United States
515-453-2080
www.strategicamerica.com

The Strategy Group LLC
United States
316-612-0300
www.thestrategygroupllc.com

Strategy Studio
United States
212-966-7800
www.strategy-studio.com

String
Serbia
38110322370

Struck
United States
801-531-0122
www.struckcreative.com

Studio Limbus
Croatia
38514818813
www.studiolimbus.com

Studio Nine Creative
United States
720-670-9040
www.studioninecreative.com

Studio Simon
United States
502-479-8447
www.studiosimon.com

studio sudar d.o.o.
Croatia
385989836579
www.iknowsudar.com

STUN Design and Advertising
United States
225-381-7266
www.stundesign.net

Stuph Clothing
United States
800-242-9166
www.stuphclothing.com

Stygar Group, Inc.
United States
804-288-4688

Subplot Design Inc.
Canada
604-685-2990
www.subplot.com

Sudduth Design Co.
United States
512-236-0678
www.sudduthdesign.com

Sunrise Advertising
United States
513-333-4100
www.sunrise-ad.com

supersoon good design
Germany
+49 40 60 73 32 94
www.supersoon.net

Sussner Design Company
United States
612-339-2886
www.sussner.com

Swanson Russell
United States
402-437-6400
www.swansonrussell.com

Synergy Graphix
United States
212-968-7568
www.synergygraphix.com

Synthetic Infatuation
United States
312-203-6267

T H Gilmore
United States
513-240-5111

T&E Polydorou Design Ltd
Cyprus
+357 24654898
www.polydoroudesign.com

Tactical Magic
United States
901-722-3001
www.tacticalmagic.com

Tactix Creative
United States
480-688-8881
www.tactixcreative.com

Tailor Designs
United States
708-843-3971
www.tailordesigns.com

Tallgrass Studios
United States
785-842-9696
www.tallgrassstudios.com

Tandem Design Agency
United States
231-946-4804
www.tandemthinking.com

Tandemodus
United States
773-927-9660
www.tandemodus.com

Tanoshism
Japan
+81 (0)80 3156 8356
www.tanoshism.com

tarsha hall design
United States
206-437-7327

Taxi Canada
Canada
403-612-9523

Taylor Design
United States
203-969-7200
www.taylordesign.com

Team Y&R
United Arab Emirates
+9714 3445444
www.yr.com

TFI Envision, Inc.
United States
203-845-0700
www.tfienvision.com

thackway+mccord
United States
212-995-1391
www.thackwayandmccord.com

Thelogoloft.com
United States
334-356-8902
www.thelogoloft.com

themarsdesign.net
United States
760-429-3692
www.themarsdesign.net

Theory Associates
United States
415-904-0995
www.theoryassociates.com

Thermostat
United States
415-250-9970
www.youaregettingwarmer.com

Thielen Designs
United States
505-205-3157
www.thielendesigns.com

Think Cap Design
United States
713-854-8873

Thinking*Room Inc.
Indonesia
628128867800
www.thinkingroominc.com

Thinkpen Design, Inc.
United States
479-306-4632

Thirtythr33
Germany
491758927118
www.thirtythr33.de

this is nido
United Kingdom
447715470235
www.thisisnido.com

Thomas Cook Designs
United States
919-274-1131
www.thomascookdesigns.com

Thread Design
China
8615000900098
www.threaddesign.com.cn

Threds
United States
865-525-2830
www.threds.com

three
United States
404-266-0899
www.3atlanta.com

Tim Frame Design
United States
614-598-0113
www.timframe.com

Timber Design Company
United States
317-213-8509
www.timberdesignco.com

Timbuktoons
United States
706-854-7704
www.timbuktoons.tv

Today
Belgium
+32 496 08 66 85
www.todaydesign.be

Todd Linkner Design Associates
United States
718-207-0682
www.toddlinkner.com

TOKY Branding+Design
United States
314-534-2000
www.toky.com

Tom Law Design
United States
404-545-0660
www.tomlawdesign.com

Toman Graphic Design
Czech Republic
420777946796
www.toman-design.com

Tomko Design
United States
602-412-4002
www.tomkodesign.com

Tomsuey Inc.
United States
212-867-5950
www.tomsuey.com

Torch Creative
United States
214-340-3938
www.torchcreative.com

Totem
Ireland
+353 58 24832
www.totem.ie

Tower of Babel
United States
503-222-9385
www.babeldesign.com

TPG Architecture
United States
212-536-5205
www.tpgarchitecture.com

Traction
United States
513-579-1008
www.teamtraction.com

Tran Creative
United States
208-664-4098
www.tran-creative.com

Trapdoor Studio
United States
602-330-2021
www.trapdoorstudio.com

Tribambuka
Russia
+7 921 3822829
www.tribambuka.com

Triple Frog LLC
United States
203-317-1042
www.triplefrog.com

TRÜF
United States
310-392-3848
www.truf.org

Truly Design
Italy
(+39) 333 338 9485
www.truly-design.com

Tyme Inc.
United States
203-594-9074
www.studiotyme.com

Type Fanatic Design
United States
480-626-3438
www.typefanatic.com

TypeOrange
United States
414-430-7030

ulitenko
Russia
+7 926 812-0388
www.ulitenko.net

UlrichPinciotti Design Group
United States
419-255-4515
www.updesigngroup.com

Ulyanov Denis
Russia
8 903 659 5304
www.caspa.ru

united*
United States
917-734-7493

UNIT-Y
United States
312-388-8864
www.unit-y.com

Urban Influence
United States
206-219-5599
www.urbaninfluence.com

UTILITY
United States
214-405-2791
www.utilitydesignco.com

Valhalla | Design & Conquer
United States
760-579-3491
www.valhallaconquers.com

Van Cyber Design
Serbia
38163386058

VanPaul Design
United States
619-793-5166
www.vanpaul.com

Vasco Morelli Design
United States
650-759-4617
www.vascomorelli.com

Velocity Design Group
United States
480-835-5535
www.velocitybrand.com

Vigor—interactive branding strategy
United States
717-234-4846
www.vigorbranding.com

VINNA KARTIKA design
Indonesia
+6281 129 8445

Vision Creative Inc.
Canada
780.452.3434

VisualCrave
United States
408-910-4553
www.visualcrave.com

visualMAFIA
Germany
498945216034
www.visualmafia.de

Vital
United Kingdom
01926 338811
www.getvital.co.uk

Vlad Ermolaev
Russia
+7 916 555 9038

vladimir sijerkovic
Serbia
381641532347
www.vladimirsijerkovic.com

volatile-graphics
United Kingdom
+44 (0)7976691230
www.volatile-graphics.co.uk

Voov Ltd.
Hungary
0036-20/33-94-922
www.voov.hu

Walsh Associates
United States
918-743-9600
www.walshbranding.com

Wantulok Design
United States
406-587-4400
www.wantulokdesign.com

Webster Design Associates Inc.
United States
402-551-0503
www.websterdesign.com

Welcome Moxie
United States
917-385-2314
www.moxiedesign.net

Westwerk DSGN
United States
612-251-4277
www.westwerkdesign.com

Weylon Smith
United States
615-306-1485
www.weylonsmith.com

WHA
United States
949-250-0607
www.whainc.com/placewrightdesign

Whaley Design, Ltd
United States
651-645-3463

Whole Wheat Creative
United States
713-993-9339
www.wholewheatcreative.com

Willoughby Design Group
816-561-4189
www.willoughbydesign.com

WONGDOODY
United States
206-624-5325
www.wongdoody.com

The Woodbine Agency
United States
336-724-0450
www.woodbine.com

Worth | Design
United States
602-499-2003

Wox
Brasil
21 24925414
www.wox.com.br

www.admarc.com
United States
888-823-6272
www.admarc.com

www.zka11.com
Bulgaria
359888835668
www.zka11.com

XYNTFK
Australia
+61 3 94158885
www.xyntfk.com

Yaroslav Zhelezniakov
Russia
7 4852 45-65-04
www.y-design.ru

Yield, Inc.
United States
512-450-5050
www.yieldinc.com

Youngha Park
United States
917-533-1804

Zed+Zed+Eye Creative Communications
United States
352-694-1933
www.zedzedeye.com

Zieldesign
United States
415-282-4040
www.zieldesign.net

Zwoelf Sonnen
Germany
1794896417
www.zwoelfsonnen.de

about the authors

Bill Gardner is president of Gardner Design in Wichita, Kansas, and has produced work for Cessna, Spirit AeroSystems, Learjet, Nissan, Thermos, Pepsi, Pizza Hut, Cargill Corporation, Kroger, Hallmark, and the 2004 Athens Olympics. His work has been featured in *Communication Arts, Print, Graphis, New York Art Directors,* the Museum of Modern Art, and many other national and international design exhibitions. He is the founder of LogoLounge.com and the author of *LogoLounge 1, 2, 3, 4* and the annual "LogoLounge: Logo Trend Reports."

Catharine Fishel specializes in working with and writing about graphic designers and related industries. Her writing has appeared in many leading publications. She is editor of the web site LogoLounge.com, contributing editor to *PRINT,* and is the author of many books about design, including *The In-House Design Handbook, The Freelance Design Handbook, Paper Graphics, Minimal Graphics, Redesigning Identity, The Perfect Package, LogoLounge 1, 2, 3, 4, 401 Design Meditations, Designing for Children, Inside the Business of Graphic Design* and *How to Grow as a Graphic Designer.*